PROJECT INTERRUPTED

LECTURES BY BRITISH HOUSING ARCHITECTS

This book presents a season of Architecture Foundation lectures by London-based architects whose practices have been strongly defined by a commitment to the design of social housing. Neave Brown and Kate Macintosh were responsible for some of the most innovative housing commissioned by local authorities in the 1960s and 1970s; Peter Barber, Farshid Moussavi and Witherford Watson Mann navigate the very different social and political conditions of today.

As our title, *Project Interrupted*, implies, these two moments of production lie to either side of a hiatus. The 1979 general election, which brought in a Conservative government led by Margaret Thatcher, effectively spelled the end of the bipartisan programme of local authority construction that had prevailed throughout the post-war years. That programme had ensured that almost 50 per cent of the population was accommodated in social housing by the mid-1970s. Now, the challenge of meeting Britain's housing needs was passed to the private sector. Local authority architect's departments were disbanded, vast swathes of public land were sold off, and millions of homes were transferred to private ownership following the dramatic expansion of the right-to-buy scheme. Even though it has long been apparent that the private sector is incapable of delivering the volume of housing that Britain's growing population requires, this new paradigm has found support from both Conservative and Labour governments for the better part of four decades.

To satisfy demand, it is estimated that the UK needs to build around 300,000 new homes each year, but the present supply stands at around half that level. Private sector developers are building fewer homes today than when Thatcher came to power. The invidious effects of the shortfall are measurable in property prices, which have rocketed beyond the reach of many of the younger generation, and in record levels of homelessness and rough-sleeping, which in some parts of the UK have quadrupled since 2010. As the Grenfell Tower fire in June 2017 made grimly clear, our housing crisis is a failure not just of supply but of quality. Socially divisive, oblivious to its urban responsibilities, mean, flimsy and unsafe, much British housing of the recent past represents a legacy unworthy of one of the richest countries in the world.

And yet there are causes for optimism, the most significant of which is the now universal recognition that the crisis is the defining political issue of the moment. Earlier this year, the Conservative MP Nick Boles acknowledged as much when he cautioned: 'This is an iceberg warning for Theresa May and the Conservative Party: if we do not take bold steps to get more houses built it will sink us at the next election.'

Regulatory changes permitting councils to retain profits from property developments are persuading a small but increasing number of them to reclaim their long-abandoned role as housebuilders. This is particularly noticeable in central London, where social housing can often be cross-subsidised by the development of homes for the open market. In the absence of the in-house architect's departments for which Neave Brown and Kate Macintosh worked, the design of this new generation of council housing is being entrusted to private practices, such as that of Peter Barber.

After decades in which cultural buildings provided the focus of the architectural discourse in the UK, housing is again moving to the top of the agenda. Opportunities for creative British architects in their home country may remain limited – as shown by Witherford Watson Mann's pursuit of commissions in Belgium, or Farshid Moussavi's work in France – but still there is a palpable sense of an industry reskilling itself, not least through a renewed interest in the achievements of the postwar years. In their recognition that the design of housing represents a negotiation between the dwelling and the city, the architects presented in this book share a purpose that transcends the obvious generational and stylistic divides. For 40 years the care and imagination which this task demands at every scale of inhabitation has been in short supply. It is very much to be hoped that we are witnessing the signs of a new beginning.

Ellis Woodman & Phineas Harper, April 2018

Neave Brown in conversation with Paul Karakusevic

NEAVE BROWN

Born in Utica, New York in 1929, Neave Brown studied at the Architectural Association in London (1950–56) and after graduating went to work for Lyons Israel & Ellis. In 1965 he completed a terrace of houses on Winscombe Street, in north London, for a group of five families, including his own. He subsequently joined the Architect's Department of the London Borough of Camden, where he delivered the Fleet Road (now Dunboyne Road) estate comprising 71 houses, a shop and studio (1975), and the Alexandra Road estate, with 520 apartments, a school, community centre, youth club and public park (1978). While all three projects have since achieved listed status, they were the last housing schemes that Brown would realise in the UK. After that, he worked on several housing schemes in the Netherlands and following the completion of the Medina at Eindhoven (2002) he retired from architecture and retrained as a printer and painter. In October 2017 the Royal Institute of British Architects awarded Neave Brown its Gold Medal in recognition of his contribution to architecture. Three weeks later he spoke to an audience of 1,300 people at an event organised by the Architecture Foundation at London's Hackney Empire. A film of that evening is available to view at www.architecturefoundation.org.uk. Neave Brown died on 9 January 2018.

Neave Brown is in conversation here with Paul Karakusevic of Karakusevic Carson Architects, which was set up to improve the quality of social housing in London. The talk took place at the Barbican Centre on 23 July 2015.

Paul Karakusevic: Neave, it has taken my practice 15 years to build just over 200 homes, whereas in seven years in Camden you managed something close to 700. What were the special conditions to make that possible?

Neave Brown: The conditions could not have been more different than they are now. What we were really working with was a post-war world. There were bombsites, masses of hoardings, but all the time we were students there was no rebuilding. London was largely destroyed, totally undecorated, unpainted, smog-laden – this was before the Clean Air Act. That was the actual physical climate we lived in. The social climate was also totally different. After all the death and destruction here was a world that longed for renewal. Bear in mind that Labour had won the 1945 election. There was the Abercrombie plan for the reconstruction of London, the Dudley Report on housing. My generation was enormously privileged. The young men who taught us had been through the war, and through them we shared in the events that had brought on the disaster. We had a new attitude. I ought to say a word or two about that attitude.

Most of the schools in England still began their teaching from the Orders. From classical models they largely progressed to the gothic and then to the English architecture of the period, which offered only a kind of a nod to modernism. The Architectural Association had no regard for that particular kind of academic set up. Our background was totally determined by interwar modernism. As students we knew every work of Le Corbusier, had every book that came out. We had Alvar Aalto, we had Mies van der Rohe, Walter Gropius, all the programmes for Frankfurt after the First World War. You can see in all this work the same strong notion of renewal – the sense of wiping out the past in order to create a totally new society.

The funny thing is that while we adored the buildings – studied their typology, took on board their aesthetics, their technology – there was a sort of reluctance to embrace the idea that we could create the world anew, from a tabula rasa. Without us being fully conscious of it, this was a growing aspect of the thinking of my group of students, people like Patrick Hodgkinson, Colin Glennie, Adrian Gale, David Gray, Ken Frampton, John Miller. Looking more closely at Le Corbusier's plan for Paris, we realised it eradicated everything but the monuments and then plonked other buildings on the levelled ground. That idea of plonking down separate buildings was also curiously present in the regulations that were coming into force in England. So we had a notion of adapting inter-war modernism to something that, without losing its quality or its spirit, would not only fit an existing environment but actively improve it, recreate it with a new kind of life. Undoubtedly one aspect of that new kind of life was social. That is to say, we hated the English class system, we hated the idea of hidden authority, we hated the idea of an elite, we hated the idea of an impoverished and undereducated poor. We wanted to create a more egalitarian society.

PK Before you arrived, Camden had been following the Corbusian model in a lot of its big rehousing programmes – a high-rise model, a tabula rasa.

NB There were two main currents in English thinking at that time. A whole lot of people thought that we shouldn't be building in cities at all, and what we needed was to create new towns everywhere that were fully planned and self-sufficient, not only in housing but in industry as well. People of that ilk loved the English countryside, adored the idea of making new kinds of communities, and rejected the old urbanity (something not unlike 1930s modernism). The other strand of thinking, which you can see in Abercrombie, was to insist that the boroughs plan every inch of the city in terms of land use, function and circulation, as well as density. The Abercrombie plan was a dense plan, with high density in the middle, reducing on the outside. It was the pyramid city.

PK Did the Abercrombie plan develop over a number of years, or was it static?

NB There were difficulties in the earlier period because the metropolitan boroughs were too small to respond to the needs for reconstruction. So in 1965 they were reorganised – Camden was a joining together of St Pancras, Holborn and Hampstead – and this reorganisation seemed automatically aligned with the kind of thinking that went with the Abercrombie plan of land use – designating functions, means of transport, and so forth. Furthermore, everything that was done in those years was done with government consent, government finance and controls. There was almost no private building. We thought of our work as projects for a new society, sponsored by the state. It was maybe naïve – certainly naïve – but that was the climate of thinking that produced not just our group, but a ten-year cohort of students.

PK That was the AA. Then in the council department, was it planning-led, or a collaboration between planners and architects?

NB When I went to Camden, the chief planner was Bruno Schlaffenberg, a planner from the Polish school who was much involved in the ideas that went with pre-war social planning, and that had to do with buildings in space, buildings that were mainly vertical, on open land with reorganised circulation systems. The chief architect, Sydney Cook – the man who hired me after seeing Winscombe Street – had very different ideas. So we fought the planners and the planners fought us. The arbiter was the political body, the council.

PK Winscombe Street might be seen as your big early break.

NB Winscombe Street was the first project I actually built. It started when I was sharing an office with the engineer Tony Hunt and we were talking about what we wanted from life. Almost simultaneously we both said that one thing we *didn't* want was to go on living in a Victorian terrace house. One day an assistant of his phoned to say that he'd found a possible site for a house, and were we interested? Tony and I went up to see it – a site at the end of Winscombe Street, a brick wall, a lot of mess behind it, a lot of green and a fantastic view down the hill.

PK Did you bring the other four neighbours together?

NB We did. Tony Hunt was one of the people we started with, but he dropped out. We were a group of five families, including, on one side of us, Michael and Patty Hopkins, and on the other, Ed Jones and his wife Beatty. We all came together and agreed that I would do the design of these houses. But the others began to feel uncomfortable when they realised that the house I was doing for them was going to be influenced by somebody else's house. 'We want a house designed for us individually', they all insisted. I had to think fast: 'I'll meet you and I'll do a design for each of you', I said, 'provided you only talk to me and don't talk to each other. That has to be an absolute rule, otherwise we'll get in a muddle.' So I had a series of very nice dinner parties with all these people, and they all talked more or less the same language because they were all more or less the same kind of people. Nobody knew precisely what they wanted, but they all chatted away. After that I designed the houses that I thought were exactly right for the site. They were all the same. Then we had more dinner parties, and I showed each person their house. They would invariably say, 'Yes, that's nice, we quite like that.' But towards the end of the evening they would get curious, 'What are the other houses like?' When they saw they were all exactly the same there was a kind of funny pause because they felt a little cheated.

So I introduced slight variations in the staircases and other details, but in essence the houses were all the same for the simple reason that this was an idea about housing. Winscombe Street wasn't serving a family, it was serving a notion about how families live together on a site. The first decision was to make the garden communal. The second was to have the children's bedrooms opening directly onto this garden. The next one was that the heart of the house would be the kitchen/dining room on the floor above, with the living and adult area on the top. I designed a house on three layers, with a terrace in the middle, overlooking the garden. That notion appealed to all the families.

PK And you borrowed money from Camden council to build the scheme?

NB That's the next thing. None of us had any money, and it was a time when councils were trying to support housing societies, so over a weekend we put ourselves together as a housing society – 'Pentad', we called it, because there were five of us. On the Monday I went to a meeting at the council offices: 'We've found this site, which is big enough for five houses, and if we build these to Parker Morris standards, exactly to the allowances the local authority will endorse, working it out with the Housing Cost Yardstick, will Camden lend us some money?' They pondered for a moment and then said, 'Yes, we will support you on that one.' Then I said, 'And furthermore we don't have enough money to buy the site. Will you lend us the money?' Again, they said yes. The only thing we had to find money for was the deposit for the site – though that was kind of difficult, as all of us were so poor at that stage. But from then on the building was financed by the London Borough of Camden and built to the social housing standards of that period – to the Parker Morris standards, which had just come in.

PK Was that the first housing coop in Camden?

NB I really don't know, I don't think so. But what I wanted to say is that there is a consistency of thinking between Winscombe Street and the larger projects. Winscombe Street is a group of five houses for people, and Fleet Road is a housing area, and Alexandra Road is, in all fairness, a piece of city. It's housing, school, community centre, building department depot, youth club, play centre, public park, integration of an adjoining estate, all continuous. However, the architectural idiom is the same all the way through these projects. There are partitions in the interiors, big sliding windows, balustrades of a certain sort (heavy wooden handrail and steel reinforcing mesh). The windows had stained softwood frames – window design was something I knew quite a lot about, because I'd done it at Lyons, Israel & Ellis.

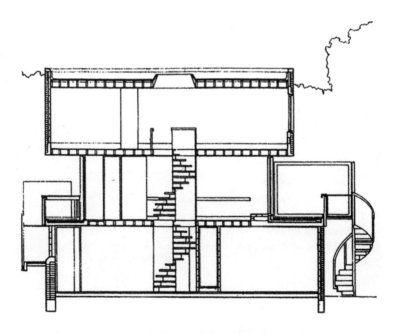

Cross section of Winscombe Street, designed 1963, completed 1965

Winscombe Street, front entrance © Mark Swenarton,
and approach from street, c 1965 © Neave Brown archive

Winscombe Street, view onto terrace from first-floor kitchen/
dining space and garden elevation © Neave Brown archive

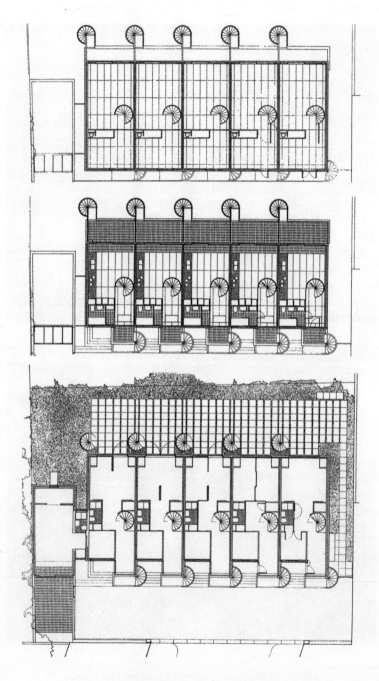

Plans of Winscombe Street, 1963–65

PK How did you find the scaling up from 5 to 70 to 500 homes, in terms of seeing the level of detail through?

NB Winscombe Street was difficult to design, but Fleet Road was a terrible operation. It was, I believe, the first high-density, low-rise scheme to get ministerial consent. Camden were eager to get as much housing as they could. The original zoning for the site – this is Abercrombie – was 130 persons per acre. Camden put it up to 160 – on a scheme that is single-storey, two-storey, three-storey, and only one of six strips is four-storey. All the roofs, apart from in the upper three strips, are terraces and open space. They all have the same proposition as Winscombe Street, of having a house with a private garden opening onto a communal space that is restricted so that children can safely play in it. So there's a thesis of land use and circulation.

PK Did you ever meet the future residents during the design process?

NB No. This is an interesting thing. We had no contact with the people at all. The idea of the double block took a long while to develop but the only person I consulted was the director of housing, a lovely man called Mr Rowley. He called me Mr Brown and I called him Mr Rowley. He found the scheme very, very difficult to understand. One of the things about Fleet Road is that it has narrow alleys down the middle, so you can have wide-fronted houses that back onto each other. We talked about these alleys, and about how they fitted into a certain kind of history of English working-class housing in the nineteenth century. We got a very nice conversation going. Then we had to show the scheme to the housing committee. All the drawings were pinned up on the walls and the committee was filing in when Rowley put his hand on my shoulder and said to me, 'Don't call them "alleys", because they'll consider that working class and they'll turn down the scheme.' So in my presentation the 'alleys' became 'passages' and the committee accepted the scheme.

PK Fantastic. The scheme seems very contextual. It fronts onto all the surrounding streets very well. Was that a big thing for you at the time? Front doors and frontages?

NB For Fleet Road? Yes, absolutely. It was to be an urban continuation. Hopefully, when you saw it on the site plan, it would look like it fitted London.

PK The huge series of estates next door – the Lismore Circus estates in Gospel Oak – are all by a collection of different architects, some

working for Camden at the time, others not. Was that quite a frustrating process to watch?

NB No, I wasn't troubled by that at all, because I did mine first. The one thing that bothered me was that people didn't seem to understand the proposition behind the work. If you are a really good dentist, people know how hard it was for you to become a dentist. If you are a really committed architect, that actual process of creation is something people don't talk about. The conversation seems limited to the obvious aspects of the shape and size of the building after the event – as if, in a curious way, there is an inevitability to them. It's very difficult, I think, to understand the problem of the conceptual process that starts with a list of requirements – a density of people, a number of cars, an adjoining building, a blank piece of paper, a blank site – all of which have to be transferred somehow or other into a proposition, which then creates the form. That was part of the thinking of our generation of architects. But for quite a long while that social aspect of the proposition was lost, and buildings returned to being simply a little lump of themselves. I think we're now recreating the notion that a building can only have a long and proper life if it has a degree of socio-cultural continuity. That idea is coming back, thank God.

PK It's very much now about working with context and the existing.

NB Yes, that's right.

PK Had you finished Fleet Road before you started on Alexandra Road?

NB Fleet Road was fully designed. But the building of it was another story. By then Camden had a well-established building department, which did all of the repair work and so on and so forth, though it had bigger ambitions. We'd gone out to tender on Fleet Road. C P Roberts, a very good contractor, submitted the lowest bid. But by that time the director of the building department had got to work on the councillors, saying that as a Labour-run council it not only had to have a building department, it had to build. So the council decided they would build Fleet Road themselves. Therefore they had to compete, so to speak, against the bids in the open tender. It was a little questionable. C P Roberts had tendered for a contract period of three years, it took Camden ten and a half. It was a nightmare, because they were totally inexperienced.

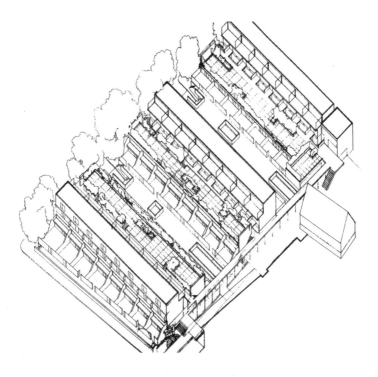

Fleet Road estate, axonometric and approach from Dunboyne Road, c 1978

Aerial view of the Fleet Road estate, looking west towards Hampstead, 1978

Fleet Road, rear terrace of Block 1 © Neave Brown archive

PK This was their first pilot project?

NB Their first building, full stop. That meant it was very slow. It was finished just around the same time as Alexandra Road. Fleet Road had 70 dwellings, Alexandra Road 520.

PK Amazing. Were they employing subcontractors, or was it all direct labour at the time?

NB They tendered out the windows, tendered out the balustrades, the usual thing. But then, for example, down those alleys, which we called passages, they laid all the drains in the wrong direction. So they had to re-lay them the right way.

PK It's reassuring to hear there were problems then as well.

NB Nobody would know that now. I shouldn't tell this story. Don't tell anybody. I'll be in terrible trouble.

PK I think we always look back through rose-tinted glasses, thinking that construction was much better.

NB And when people see buildings, they don't on the whole know the drama behind them, do they?

PK No. But the build quality inside your maisonette is now very, very good.

NB Well, it has some cracks and funny things. Camden had a 'Better Homes' programme, which required changes to everything from the kitchens to the whole structure of the building. I won't comment on that, except to say it was really rather difficult. They replaced all the windows, for instance, with the same kind of windows that we'd designed for them. So what was the point of that?

PK Moving on to Alexandra Road, is it right that there was a previous scheme for the site?

NB The planners would do design layouts, and Alexandra Road had the railway running all the way along the north wall. It was the main line to Euston then, and had more traffic on it than it does now. The noise of the railway, together with the decay of the existing houses, was the reason why Camden could buy the whole 16-acre site relatively cheaply. The first decision they had to take was whether to restore the houses, or rebuild. Rebuilding allowed them to push up the density to 160 persons to the acre. To maintain this density, two of the planned four acres of public park were incorporated into the open space for the housing. They'd done a diagram of lumps of building on the site, which was the way people did things then. Honourable stuff, but a diagram all the same. So that was what we inherited. Camden then decided – because the need was so great – to add a school for mentally handicapped children. Then we added a community centre and shopping. Then the building department – the same one we were struggling with at Fleet Road – needed a depot. So all of this stuff came pouring in together with the integration of the adjoining estate, making for the most incredibly complex brief. Rather than interpreting these different elements simply as lumps of building, to be arranged nicely on the site, the notion was to make a continuous environment that belonged to the urban environment of London. That was the kind of idea that was prevailing in my generation – not just me. All of those pieces had not just to be next to each other; they had to adjoin, to enhance each other in function and use. So the community centre, for instance, is linked to the halls and kitchens for the school below, while the playground at the back of the school opens directly into the youth club, so the kids could all play together. Everything on Alexandra Road is not just a continuous form; it's a notion of continuous, mutually enhancing function. It sounds pretentious, but it's just the idea of making things work together.

PK How long did that process take? Developing the brief and then the early design?

NB You start with a blank piece of paper and you draw the site. The site has a huge list of accommodations. Alexandra Road follows the discontinuous curve of the railway – straight, curve, straight, curve. I love that beautiful curve of the railway. The planners also required pedestrian and vehicle segregation, which I endorsed, though I have mixed feelings about it. Then there's your own thinking. From the very start I wanted to make a street, so in one sense the diagram of the long street happened quite quickly, but then you have to work and work and work to make something out of it.

You know what this is like. You stand back and say, 'Oh my God, what can I do with that?' Then you go back the next day: 'What about that back section of the road? How to get the buildings close together? How to ensure they all have light? And have every front door relate to the street? And give every living room an open space – something that's not just a balcony, but part of the building? Gradually something develops and you get all these things working together, to give an overall kind of notion about the mass. Then something else has to be done to turn all this into architecture. You draw and draw and draw.

PK We do a lot of redrawing.

NB What I'm building up to saying is that in the end, when you've got it right, and they build it, it looks inevitable. The struggle to produce what you produce has disappeared. That process, though I'm talking about it tonight, on the whole is almost never talked about.

To do Alexandra Road, we relied on a genius of a quantity surveyor, Neil Kenworthy, a man of amazing ability. We did what is called two-stage tendering, where we designed the building with all sorts of technical situations in it and gave contractors the option of suggesting how to do things within geometric limits. We had C P Roberts, who were going to precast all the elements in an on-site factory, and another contractor, McInerney, who wanted to do everything in situ – they had a large, highly trained labour force that they'd been developing over years. Their prices were almost exactly the same, but McInerney had an advantage in terms of the programming, because C P Roberts would have needed time first to make their factory. So we chose McInerney, and changed our working drawings in consultation with them. Then there was the longest pause, because a whole year was lost over a road-closing inquiry. We eventually got the right decision, and sat down for our first site meeting. I remember it still. I sat there on one side with my people, the structural engineers and so forth, and on the other side was the McInerney contingent, with Mr Bugler and Mr O'Brien, flanked by two or three rather powerful-looking people. Mr Bugler got straight to the point, 'We're subcontracting all the concreting

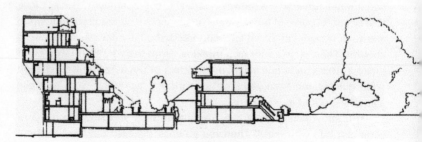

Neave Brown, section of Alexandra Road with (from left)
housing Blocks A, B and C, designed 1968, built 1973–78

to a major concreting firm.' And, lo and behold, that firm wanted to go back to precasting some of the elements. There was no question, at that moment, of saying that this was totally unacceptable. I had to agree to it there and then, knowing that we'd have to redo all the drawings.

PK How big was the team at that point?

NB That was another issue. Alexandra Road was a very big, complicated project – altogether, it added up to eight buildings, plus the additional parking, plus the landscape. We worked out that at its peak we would need up to 12 people, including administrators.

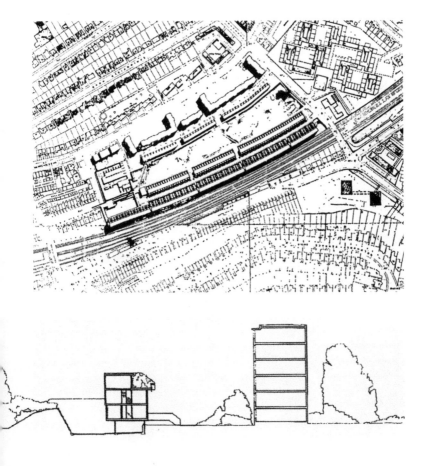

Alexandra Road, site plan © Neave Brown archive

Alexandra Road, park between Blocks B and C: in the foreground, under construction, the play centre designed by Kisa Kawakami

Alexandra Road, playgrounds in park, landscaping by Janet Jack (above) and central street between Blocks A and B (right)

Alexandra Road, rear and front of Block A © Neave Brown archive

PK Very efficient.

NB Yes, but we had just seven people, then eight. We asked Sydney Cook to demand more staff from the council. They refused. So there we were, committed to a contract, to a budget, with major changes to make – the concrete wasn't the only one. The year's delay had also given the district surveyor and his inspectors the opportunity to decide that they no longer approved of the timber roof for the school, which was overhung by some concrete elements. So we had to change the roof of the school back to concrete.

PK At the last minute.

NB At the very last minute. Which meant, of course, different loading. All the foundations, the whole structure underneath the parking, had to be changed too, just when the contractor wanted to start the build.

PK A sure recipe for success.

NB Fortunately, you begin with foundations, don't you? Well, the first year was almost all underground; the second year, columns started coming up. At most, we had nine people, and I've never seen a group of people work as hard as they did. We'd got an extraordinary spirit going with that building.

PK And the relationship with the main contractor and the subcontractors, was that a good collaboration?

NB We had a very good relationship with McInerney, though my God, we had our conflicts. But talk about a good spirit. A lot of us – Max Fordham and I included – would always cycle to the site. One day I challenged Max to race down the road – of course he was much stronger than I was. We had this race, and then McInerney, the contractor, suggested that we make it an annual event. So for the rest of the years it took to build that building we had the Great Alexandra Road Bicycle Race.

PK Along the street?

NB No, McInerney worked out a nightmare of a route, carrying the bike up a ladder, along scaffolding, down a slope, across a muddy area, through a wet patch. Every year they excelled in inventing devilish new twists to challenge us. Everyone joined in – the architects, the consultants, some of their people, some of our children.

PK I heard there was a flood in the early stages of Alexandra Road.

NB On a building like that you are bound to have problems. For instance, the whole of B block lived on strip foundations. All the core studies had been taken to test the soil and at a certain depth they showed a soft layer of blue clay, not that thick, a little squashed out. When we came to build the first building we were above that. Then we went down the site and hit this blue clay, which we had to go below. But we could only lower the foundations so far before we had to stop and think again. The redesign of the foundations set us back about seven months. Then, when we got going again, we had to deal with a Victorian sewer – one of the major ones, carrying the sewage from Hampstead Hill, came under the railway and under our site. We had a long discussion with Camden Water Board about how to do it. We agreed to bridge the sewer with concrete foundations and beams and then encase the top part of the brick structure in a six-inch layer of concrete. The problem was the Water Board's rule that we had to do all of this without disturbing the existing cover. 'How's that possible?', we asked. 'We can't allow you to remove the cover', they again insisted, 'but we won't look at the sewer for one weekend'. So we set the whole thing up to be done over a single weekend. We had a range for the concreting and McInerney brought in the most expert diggers I've ever seen in my life. My God, they dug with precision. We removed all the cover from that sewer on a Friday – and then it started to rain, the heaviest rain on record at that time. Then the district surveyor turned up and said, 'We can't allow you to concrete in these conditions.' We had masses of concrete and all of these huge machines, all of these people standing around ready to go, and suddenly everything had to stop. I rang the following morning to see how things were, and they told me, 'Mr Brown, you'd better come along to the site.' What had happened was that the water had come down from Hampstead Hill and, for the only time in history, had filled to capacity the beautiful egg-shaped Victorian sewer – and blown it up. We had a fountain in the middle of that site. It was rather beautiful, though the flooding set us back again. Anyway, you'll have stories like this too.

PK We have a few. Only they're not quite so dramatic.

NB That was indeed a drama. There were these two men standing by the bubbling water. One had a briefcase and bowler hat, and one had an umbrella. They were Water Board people. What could I say to them? I tried, 'My God, what on earth do you do when this sort of thing happens?' One of them said, 'This has never happened before.' The other one looked at me and said, 'It will never happen again.' It was an amazing thing. But on a big, big site like that, you'll have a series of dramas all the way through. You just have to deal with them as they happen.

PK It's an incredible feat with a team of eight or nine people.

NB Then there was the fact that they started the white concrete with their own mix, which started to go pink. We had to stop them and insist they use the mix we had invented, adapting their own mix in stages so the contrast didn't show. We also had the worst ever period of inflation in the building industry in London. There were problems with labour: the skilled workers were going into the programmes to satisfy the tourist industry, a whole series of hotels. McInerney simply couldn't compete. We ended up having to change the contract and go onto a cost-trust basis. Instead of three and a half years, it took five years to finish.

PK By which time Sydney Cook had...

NB ... left Camden and Alf Rigby had come in. At our first meeting I told him I was in definite need of support, especially with the contract management, because we simply couldn't cope with all the paperwork. He agreed immediately and we got two more architecture staff, and people to help with the management. The people who worked in the office for me were fantastic. But because of all of this, and because of the inflation – and not because of any kind of incompetence – the building took a great deal longer and cost more, which caused a huge political problem. But anyway, you know about that kind of thing too.

PK We always have one or two political problems. One more question. At the moment, unlike when you finished at the AA and went into the council department, a lot of the young architects graduating now are setting up their own practice very early, with a renewed interest in the public sector. Have you got any advice for that new generation coming through?

NB I have no advice. As an architect, in my opinion, you're always trying to put together two things. You have your client's agenda – there will be certain kinds of spaces and requirements, a little money. Then you'll have what I've always called the hidden agenda, some of which you share with the client as the project develops and some of which he never knows about. You want to put these things together, not just in terms of function but in terms of the environment, the life of the building, the neighbours, the spirit of the thing, different attitudes to flexibility and mix and so forth. But it isn't the architect who pays for the building, who sets the brief, it's the client who does that. He expresses his need, and with some reluctance he has to go to a bloody architect to get it built. Now we were able to do what we wanted to do because our hidden agenda – which was the social, political, aesthetic one from the modern movement – happened to be in sympathy with the dominant political attitudes at that time. I think it's very difficult for an architect to have a complex set of social, cultural, aesthetic propositions that are acceptable within the processes you have to adhere to now. For instance, when I was doing it, the architect worked directly with the client. Now, on large buildings, the architect frequently works with a management consultant who's not interested in the subtleties of a hidden agenda – he's interested in money and time and a very, very minimal notion of function compared to the complex ideas that we were able to play with. Now it is much more overtly about the declared need of the client, as run by management.

PK And spreadsheets.

NB And that gives far fewer options. Does that accord with your experience, or am I exaggerating? I don't know.

PK I think things are changing now. Local councils are much more ambitious than they were a few years ago.

NB It's getting back to the stage where more complicated issues are addressed.

PK They are brave enough to now push forward again.

NB Undoubtedly, because it did go through a very bad period, didn't it?

PK For 35 years, there was really no housing designed. So it is the beginning of something. You feel that spirit in some of the council departments now. One final question before we open up to the floor. When the residents moved in to Alexandra Road, what was their reaction to the completed project?

NB I need to put this in a little context. The council that committed to Alexandra Road in 1967 was Labour, but by the time it was finished in 1979 the council had changed a couple of times – first to Tory, then back to Labour. But by this time Mr Rowley had retired. The new housing department was suspicious of Alexandra Road to the same degree that the previous ones had supported it. They advised a new council that the scheme would be a catastrophe and a disaster. In response, the council made a political move to distance itself from Alexandra Road, announcing a public inquiry even before it was finished. That was the atmosphere towards the end, and it came out in nit-picking arguments over all sorts of funny things.

It's true that the construction site looked pretty messy when the new council officers saw it for the first time. McInerney were lovely Irish builders, but my God they were untidy – they left broken ladders about the place and boxes of things that should have been carried away. Then suddenly, in the last few months of construction, McInerney cleaned it all up. They polished the floors and cleaned the glass and did the last bits of decoration – painted the blue, blue and the red, red – and it looked marvellous. Camden had been worried that nobody would want to live there, but when they opened it for letting, people were queuing up. The first block was occupied. The people who moved in loved it: they competed to see who could do the best garden on their terrace. By that time, of course, the public inquiry had spelled the end of my professional life in England.

PK That was a wonderful hour and more. Thank you very much, Neave. Are there any questions from the floor?

Q1 I live in Alexandra Road. Thank you very much for building my home, I think it's wonderful. I'd like to ask about the white concrete, which is beautiful in all the pictures taken soon after completion. Obviously it's not so white now.

NB It looks terrible.

Q1 What was your intention when you built it?

NB The only way we could do the building was in concrete, so we worked out how to do it with ordinary concrete on the inside and this white concrete on the outside. At that stage, I was in close contact with all the people at Camden who dealt with maintenance. The idea was that the concrete would be cleaned regularly, in terms of partial cleaning, and there would be a programme set up for proper maintenance and intensive cleaning as required. Then, of course, there were all the cuts to the council's budget, which restricted its ability to look after its buildings – and Alexandra Road was not alone in that. There has been no attention to the concrete, so it has just got blacker and blacker. Likewise, the rendering that you see now looks patchy and terrible. We had agreed to do the rendering as they used to do it at the turn of the eighteenth/nineteenth century, where you have a soft rendering that's done with a certain kind of mix that is then left to cure for five years before it's painted. That was the mild white rendering that we were going to have on Alexandra Road. Again, it was well understood between us as architects and the Camden people. Of course, in the event they never painted it. The rendering is cracked in places, and it's got blotchy and pieces have fallen off.

Q2 Fascinating talk. Following on from your comment about surveys informing your design decisions (or not), I wonder how you feel about the current interest in engaging local people in the design of community facilities and housing. You mentioned there was no consultation on Winscombe Street, for example.

NB Again let me put this in some context. At the time we were designing Alexandra Road, there was no question of consultation because there was nobody to consult with – it was a totally cleared site. Then after the final change in the Camden housing department I had a series of meetings with the new council officials who came along and said, 'We've done surveys so we know where people want the kitchen. It's next to the front door, and certainly not upstairs in the furthest corner of the living room. Almost none of the things that you've done on Alexandra Road, according to our surveys, are what people want.' For me, those surveys didn't satisfy any of the criteria for a legitimate 'consultation'.

However, if you work with a group to create a sense of order that is not imposed but agreed, where they accept that not everything they want can be fulfilled because the building is going to live for 40, 50 or 60 years and it has got to have all sorts of values in it – if you can do that, then consultation can certainly work. But when it doesn't work, you can end up with frustration. So you have to be careful how you set it up and how the authority then works within it. I'm not experienced in that and you are, Paul. You can talk about that.

PK In every single project now there's probably anything between 5 and 50 consultation events with existing residents or residents who will be rehoused in the new homes.

NB I never had to do it.

PK I think with experience you learn what to ask, or sometimes what not to ask. It's very much part of the creative process now.

Q3 HS2 is coming underneath us: is the building going to fall down?

NB No. That's been carefully studied. I don't think HS2 should go underneath, but as far as I know it won't bring the building down.

PK There are a few engineers in the room. Maybe they can advise later.

NB If it does fall down, I hope I'm young enough to do another building.

Q4 Neave, you recount these tales with supreme confidence. With the hindsight of 40 years, what you were achieving was extremely bold. Did you ever have any doubts about Alexandra Road and whether what you were proposing was the right thing?

NB It's a difficult question to answer, because I had incredible, intense doubts all the time I was doing it. I wondered whether I had the authority to do those bedrooms and sliding doors, or that all-in-one living room–dining–kitchen. But I'd worked with those ideas before and as the proposition developed I achieved a kind of cumulative confidence. I think we all know that feeling. You know you're imposing an order, but you're hoping it's one that is flexible enough for people to live within. You go through this difficult, disciplined, irregular, unknown, faulty, do-it-again, do-it-again process to arrive at what you end up with. And nobody notices, but in a curious way that's alright, because the thing has inevitably become what it is – a normal place to live.

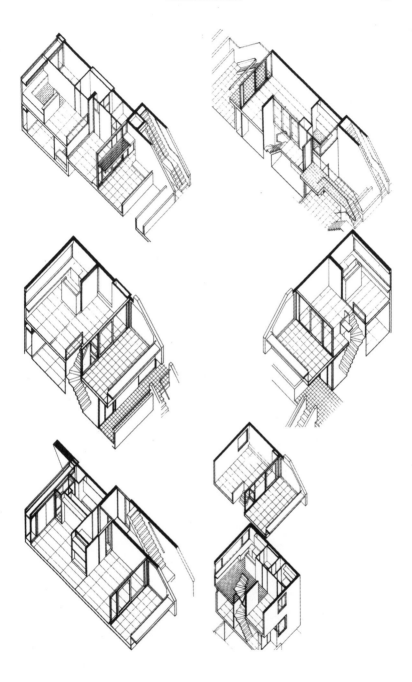

Axonometric drawing of two-, three- and four-person units at Alexandra Road

These pages: Alexandra Road, interior views shortly after completion, 1978
© Neave Brown archive

Overleaf: Side of Block A from Abbey Road
© Neave Brown archive

PETER BARBER

Peter Barber (b 1960) studied under David Greene at the Polytechnic of Central London and worked with Richard Rogers, Will Alsop and Jestico+Whiles prior to establishing Peter Barber Architects in 1989. In 2001 the firm won first prize in the Architecture Foundation-run competition for the Donnybrook Quarter (2006), a development of 40 homes commissioned by the housing association Circle 33 for a site in Hackney. Barber's close-packed, highly articulated terraces capitalised on recently published legislation directed towards achieving a significant increase in housing densities in urban areas – Planning Policy Guidance 3: Housing (2000). Donnybrook set a template for a low-rise, street-based urbanism that his practice has continued to explore through projects such as Tanner Street Gateway in Barking (2007) and Worland Gardens in Stratford (2017). Barber is currently a lecturer and reader in architecture at the University of Westminster. The talk took place at the Royal Geographical Society on 24 May 2017.

There are numerous ways to approach the design of housing, lots of hats that we can and should wear – abstract and analytical, political, sensual, social, artistic, pragmatic even. We need to be sociologist, geographer, architect and urbanist – old-style masterplanner and situationist both.

I'd like to start with a series of preambles that aim to tease out the ideological and political context for our work. These quotes, images and observations capture the atmosphere and ethos of what we do and in a sense provide a moral compass for our design process. I'll then move on to describe how these ideas find expression in three of our built projects and in '100-Mile City', our theoretical proposal for a street-based linear city encircling London.

ONE

'Perhaps the most democratic achievement of elected government in the twentieth century was the building of council housing to let at rent that the workers could afford. The endeavour was the essence of social democracy. It was socialist because it favoured the poor and it was democratic because the landlord was the elected authority responsible to the tenant.' —Paul Foot, *The Vote*, 2005

The UK was broke in the aftermath of the Second World War, and yet successive governments still found the resources not only to fund the National Health Service but to build 150,000 homes annually.

By 1975, nearly half the population enjoyed the benefits of living in council housing. In the intervening years, this policy has been reversed with a series of disastrous housing acts. Governments of both political complexions have abandoned their commitment to social housing. Since 1979, HALF of all public-owned land has been sold into private ownership and two million homes have been sold, at heavily discounted prices, under the nonsensical 'right-to-buy' scheme. Today, only around eight per cent of the population lives in council housing.

Consequently in London alone there are currently: 170,000 homeless people (Shelter's robust minimum figure); 8,000 rough sleepers, a total that has doubled in the last four years; 20,000 empty homes; and 150 families losing their home each day. At the same time we have seen an exponential rise in property prices and the cost of private-sector rentals – 259 per cent over the course of the last 10 years.

'Post-war estates across the country are ripe for redevelopment...
we will sweep away the planning blockages and take new steps to reduce
political and reputational risk for projects' key decision-makers and investors.
I believe that together we can tear down anything that stands in our way.'
— David Cameron, Estate Regeneration, 10 January 2016

In my view, housing is basic infrastructure and *not* a commodity, and the control of the land economy and housing production has to be a matter for government – much as it was in the middle part of the last century.

Three simple policies would decommodify housing and end the housing crisis: 1. Introduce private-sector rent controls; 2. Halt the selling of council houses under 'right-to-buy'; 3. Build 150,000 council houses a year funded by direct taxation.

It would be interesting to reflect on ways in which this new wave of council housing production might be devolved, bottom up, or incremental.

Street bed / 25 million pound apartment

TWO

'The passion for improvisation ... demands that space and opportunity be at any price preserved. Buildings are used as a popular stage. They are all divided into innumerable simultaneously animated theatres. Balcony, courtyard, window, gateway, staircase, roof are at the same time stages and boxes ... as porous as the stone is the architecture. Buildings and action interpenetrate in the courtyards, arcades and stairways. In everything they preserve the scope to become a theatre of new unforeseen constellations. The stamp of the definitive is avoided. No situation appears intended forever.' —Walter Benjamin, *One Way Street*, 1924

Walter Benjamin's description of the culture and form of a street in Naples captures beautifully the idea of a city animated by the activities of its occupants – by a spatiality that is permeable, that invites occupation. He gives us an intimation of the fragile and complex reciprocal relationship that exists between people and space, between culture and architecture. His message: without people and culture, space is inert.

Our projects work with the idea that space conditions and is in turn conditioned by society and culture, and that architecture can create the potential for social action and activity. I always find it helpful to visualise how people might inhabit the spaces that we create and I love revisiting our built housing projects to see how people's lives are played out in their homes and in the courtyards and on the streets we have made.

A popular stage: a street market in Naples

THREE

Housing accounts for 70 per cent of all the buildings in London. It's what our city is made of. It's what creates a hard edge to our streets, what surrounds our squares.

Therefore when we design urban housing we are designing cities. Designs for housing should begin as urban designs, driven in the first instance by our vision of a beautiful city. Projects like Donnybrook Quarter contain housing but more fundamentally they are a celebration of the life of the city.

Personalised front doors in the Donnybrook Quarter

FOUR

I'm for street-based neighbourhoods. Streets are an ingenious and effective means of organising public space. Axial streets especially, being easy to understand and navigate, can help to create a city that is well integrated, both spatially and socially.

Picture the experience of a stroll along The Laine in Brighton, an un-remarkable but successful street with characteristics we can learn from:

— It is well integrated into the spatial fabric of the city, as part of network of streets that make the city permeable and provide strong visual and spatial connections between adjacent yet socially diverse neighbourhoods.
— It is narrow, concentrating the public life of the area into a very limited space. It brings together people of diverse social, economic and cultural groups and creates the potential for a colourful social scene.
— The buildings that bound the street house a mix of uses – retail, leisure, business and residential – that create a vibrant local culture and 24-hour occupancy.
— There is a strong visual connection between the buildings themselves and the street. This means that every inch of public space is overlooked or naturally policed. It is hard to imagine a mugging or robbery taking place here.
— Narrow building frontages and numerous front doors create visual diversity and the potential for occupiers to personalise their space.

The Laine, Brighton

Pitfield Street, London

Now compare this to Pitfield Street, in East London, where you walk 50m up the street and turn right through a gap between buildings to enter a very different world – the vast hinterland of inter- and post-war housing estates that stretches across Hoxton. The designers of these estates eschewed the street in favour of a spatiality that has blighted the lives of thousands of residents for three generations:

— The spaces between buildings create no useful routes across this part of the city, forcing people to make lengthy and inconvenient detours around them.
— Dead ends, blind alleyways, burnt-out garages, paladin stores block off any views into, or routes across, the estates. Concealed from view in this way, one of London's most socially disadvantaged areas has become segregated from the rest of the city – a ghetto.
— The estates are laid out as a series of objects dotted around in acres of unused space: some concrete pavers or tarmac here, a patch of grass there. Such large, dispersed spaces tend to dissipate social activity, limiting the potential for people to meet or even to see fellow residents. Deserted most of the time, they create an environment which tends to isolate people and increase their vulnerability to crime. Some on the estate are afraid to leave their apartments. Most affected are the elderly, racial minorities and women.

Against this, I like to try and arrange our projects as a network of streets often interspersed with little public squares and gardens. I aim to align streets so that they create handy shortcuts and strong spatial and visual connections with adjacent neighbourhoods.

I like to imagine narrow streets which concentrate the public world into a fairly limited space, bringing together lots of different types of people. And it's nice to think of narrow building frontages and numerous front doors creating visual diversity and the potential for people to personalise the space outside their home.

Le Corbusier said *'a street is linear factory'* – typically hyperbolic. But it's good to think of a productive city, houses over workshops, shop windows and loading bays, clobber at the kerb, messy cross-programming – pre-war London, Marrakesh, Old Delhi.

FIVE

I am interested in medium-rise, higher-density housing, and often try to explore the possibility of achieving this with houses instead of flats.

We like to experiment with unconventional housing typologies. Some of them are quite obscure or belong to a pre-modern vernacular – the Tyneside or cottage flat, back-to-back houses, courtyard house types, double and treble stack 'walk ups' – not to mention the hybrid terrace/courtyard notched terrace, which I nicked from Adolf Loos and Jose Luis Sert.

Where higher-rise apartments are required it seems to me that pre-modern tenement housing and mansion block typologies are a good model. They define a clear and unambiguous edge to the street, and tend to concentrate circulation within the street itself, with numerous and regular points of street access and minimal interior circulation – think also of Neave Brown's Alexandra Road.

SIX

Sergei Eisenstein said that Greek urbanists were the first great cinematographers.

While I'm designing I sometimes try to imagine our schemes as a screenplay, a sequence of views, long, lyrical tracking shots, a shocking jump cut, Sergio Leone-style shifts in scale from detail to widescreen panorama – silhouette, close up, perspective shifting, space unfolding, picturesque, sensual – a shadowy street with a little kick, tapering and narrowing suddenly before opening through an archway into the corner of a sunny square ... mmm, nice!

It's good in this context to think also of Debord's situationist *dérive* and psychogeographic maps, or Baudelaire's *flâneur* – the city and its streets understood and experienced 'on the ground', at eye level.

SEVEN

I love straight streets in grids – stretched, square, diamond, triangular, hexagonal grids. Let's take a look at the possibilities.
— Thin, gregarious grids, slivers of terraced houses pushed up to the kerb – brash, showy, public – Brighton, Barceloneta, back-to-back Brum, Western-set thin, city of pleasure, city of the body, city as theatre, building as backdrop.
— Or what about a deep, square grid, a modest, introverted, reflective city of blocks and courtyards – Oxford, Fez.
— Or a triangular grid with 60-degree corners – a city of flows, gentle changes of direction, seductive, democratic even.

EIGHT

Djemaa el Fna, the extraordinary public square embedded in the medieval walls of Marrakesh, in my view exemplifies what public space is – or at least what it can be.

Like all public space it is unique because it belongs at the same time to no one and to everyone – to old and young, rich and poor, tourists and locals alike. It's a place where people can express themselves with relative freedom.

Djemaa el Fna has no monuments and is almost entirely surrounded by unexceptional buildings. For much of the day it remains fairly quiet. However in the cool of the evening the teeming alleyways of the old town spill into it and a tumultuous scene unfolds.

Little mobile kitchens appear from nowhere, people form circles around fire-eaters, acrobats and story-tellers. Theatre troupes perform on hastily erected stages. There are snake charmers and oud players, drum bands and fireworks. This is an architecture of festivity, ephemeral, mobile, in flux – foregrounded by people, its message embodied in its name: Djemaa el Fna translates as '*Mosque of Nothing*'. I love the idea of public space being a 'mosque of nothing': open, unprogrammed, where people can be themselves.

Behind the photographer is Djemaa el Fna's antithesis, the Grand Mosque of Marrakesh – metre-thick walls, solid, immutable, unchanging.

NINE

In *The Practice of Everyday Life* Michel de Certeau says that space is 'practised place', 'everyday narrative', 'a word caught in the ambiguity of actualisation', 'on streets, in apartments and in the most intimate of domestic habits'.

It's useful to think about small things, everyday habits, domestic rituals, the turning of a door handle, footsteps on the stairs, the view from a window seat.

Peter Zumthor zooms in like this: 'I remember the sound of gravel under my feet, the soft gleam of the waxed oak staircase...'

Our Gadget Apartment celebrates everyday things and ordinary domestic rituals. It is homespun, assembled from oddments found in local skips, tips and junk shops, stuff left lying around. Cheap, handy, bespoke, the residue of previous construction and destruction.

— *Mono-gold door* At the threshold between the public world and the apartment interior the inside face of the front door is covered in gleaming squares of gold leaf found in a junk shop.
— *Bath tidy* Copper pipe wraps the bathroom wall as radiator, towel rail and handy hook for razor, soap dish and toothbrush. No home should be without one!
— *Tap and soap dish* A tap assembled from bits of old taps and a spiral coat-hanger wire soap dish.

— *Match shelf* A tiny wire shelf so you know where your matches are.
— *Wok-hob* Two second-hand wok burners and some mesh out of a skip.
— *Metachron B1 table* (with Ben Stringer) A dining table assembled from
a triangle of broken glass and three traffic cones, all found in the street.

Match shelf and Metachron B1 table

TEN

In the 1950s the Corporation of Great Yarmouth embarked on the destruction of the town's historic centre, 35 acres of tiny streets and alleys known as the Yarmouth Rows, home and workplace to over 18,000 people – extraordinary architecture, Elizabethan and Georgian, but in their view *'an insanitary and utterly unsatisfactory form of development which could not possibly be retained'*.

Slum clearance programmes like this resulted in the demolition of vast quantities of back-to-back and terraced housing in the Midlands and the North of England, the sweeping away of serviceable and popular tenements in Glasgow and Edinburgh, the bulldozing of great swathes of street-based housing from Brighton to Newcastle.

Sixty years on, the same functionalist planning culture still prevails, favouring a dispersed, suburban, anti-social spatiality. Tick-box policy enforced through generic design standards, overlooking distances, car parking minimums, idiotic daylight, sunlight and air-quality indicators. Urbanism measured in habitable rooms/hectare, decibels, square metres, lux.

I would like to see radical new planning policy designed to encourage compact, continuous, urban form – a densely packed, convivial, congested city of intimately scaled streets and alleys where people from all different backgrounds could live alongside one another, where narrow streets compress and intensify the urban and human experience. In short, a socially and ecologically sustainable urbanism structured by idealism, rather than net-twitch neurosis.

Street party, Great Yarmouth Row 116, 1935

DONNYBROOK QUARTER

Donnybrook Quarter is a lower-rise, medium-density, street-based city quarter located on a prominent corner site just south of Victoria Park in Hackey, East London. Its starting point is urban, aiming to provide well-used public space, bounded by a hard edge of buildings.

The scheme is laid out around two new tree-lined streets that cross the site, creating very strong spatial connections with adjacent neighbourhoods and a handy cut through for their residents.

The streets have an intimate scale, being 7.5m wide and bordered on each side by two- and three-storey buildings. At their intersection – the heart of the scheme – the two streets widen into a tree-lined square.

Balconies, terraces, oriel windows and numerous front doors animate the facades of the buildings, creating private spaces that overhang or overlap the street. This is a place for deckchairs, colourful plants and laundry – maybe even for people to come together.

At the southern end of the site, where they meet Old Ford Road, the buildings rise to four storeys and non-residential uses are introduced – two shops and a café. At the eastern edge, an elegant residential terrace follows the gentle curve of Parnell Road.

The housing employs an unusual courtyard–terrace hybrid typology. The typical double unit has a two-bed flat at ground level and a two-bed maisonette on the two floors above. The notched terrace configuration enabled us to achieve densities of 520 habitable rooms per hectare while maintaining high levels of privacy and amenity to every dwelling. Each dwelling has its own front door onto the street and a 4m by 8m courtyard.

The upper maisonette is entered from the street via a staircase leading to a courtyard garden at first floor. The living area has a fully glazed sliding screen that faces south, over the courtyard. Upstairs there is a double bedroom, a second bedroom or study, a bathroom and a balcony that overlooks the street.

In the ground-floor flat the front door opens directly into an open-plan living area. The room is flooded with light from a fully glazed sliding screen, which gives access to a courtyard garden to the rear. The living area leads to a double bedroom, a single bedroom or study and a bathroom. The courtyard in each dwelling is an unprogrammed or 'slack space' that we hope might be used by residents needing a 'lean to', greenhouse, outdoor gym, paddling pool or garden – you name it.

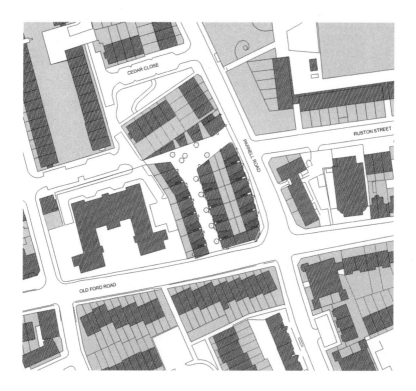

Site plan and view from northwest © Morley von Sternberg

Pedestrian street looking north and view from southeast © Morley von Sternberg

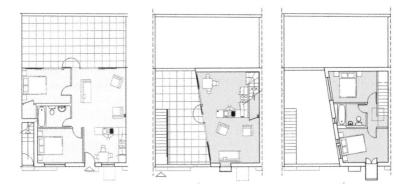

Plan of typical unit and view of courtyard © Morley von Sternberg

BEVERIDGE MEWS

Beveridge Mews is a row of eight terraced houses and a new community garden, including a children's play area, located within the Stepney Green Estate in Tower Hamlets, East London. It is 100 per cent affordable housing.

Tower Hamlets has high levels of poverty and a great need for social housing. In particular there is under-provision of housing for extended families and a significant problem of overcrowding within individual homes. Beveridge Mews seeks to address this shortage by providing houses that are designed to accommodate large, multi-generational families and range in size from four to six bedrooms. In allocating homes, priority was given to existing Stepney Green residents.

The project is laid out as a beautifully landscaped garden square. Our building is configured as a thin, notched terrace ranged along the western boundary of the site; the three remaining sides of the square are formed by existing housing. The new housing is clad in timber shingles, referencing the 'make do and mend' aesthetic of the existing garden sheds and patchwork of garden fences of the building opposite. Its complex stepped profile is designed to provide sunny spots for people to hang out and do stuff. Already we've seen a little outdoor gym, a whirly gig, bikes being fixed, a sun lounger and tomato plants – just as we'd hoped.

The thin, notched terrace of Beveridge Mews

Garden square and view of southwest corner © Morley von Sternberg

HOLMES ROAD STUDIOS

Holmes Road Studios is a homeless facility located in North London. It provides high-quality residential accommodation together with training and counselling facilities, all laid out around a new courtyard garden.

The courtyard is defined at its north end by the existing Victorian Dutch-gabled hostel building containing shared facilities and conventional hostel accommodation. The other three sides are formed by 30 little studio houses arranged as terraces in an almshouse typology.

Each cottage is 16m² in area and consists of a double-height, brick-vaulted living/kitchen/dining area and, at the back of the plan, a bathroom with a mezzanine bed space raised above it. The interior is lit via a partially glazed door, circular windows and a roof light. The use

Holmes Road Studios, central garden

of a rustic-looking brick with a crinkle-crankle parapet gives the project a relaxed domestic scale. All of the rooms look out over the garden, which will become a therapeutic project for the benefit of residents.

We imagine a group of residents working with a gardener to create and maintain an intensely planted and beautiful garden, with an apple tree or two, potatoes, green veg, soft fruit, herbs, a greenhouse, a potting shed and a sunny spot to sit and rest. We think there ought to be a little room/shed in the garden for private chats (1:1) and counselling. Conceived as the social heart of the hostel, the garden creates a homely, domestic atmosphere. It gives participating residents an interest and outlet for their energy, helping to foster a sense of belonging, self-worth and empowerment.

Holmes Road Studios, axonometric view and elevation © Morley von Sternberg

100-MILE CITY

100-Mile City is a necessary and provocative response to the 2015 report from the Adam Smith Institute which insisted that 'London's Green Belt must be built on to curtail the housing crisis'. The project is a work in progress but currently takes the form of a plaster model and drawings by Peter Barber Architects and a film, 'The True History of the Hundred Mile City', directed by Grant Gee.

Build a street-based, linear city 100 miles long, 100 metres wide and four storeys high. Wrap it round London. Give it little factories, schools, houses and shops laid out in terraces along intimately scaled streets and around squares. Make it a dense, intense edge to London – a confident, purposeful boundary fronting a revitalised productive countryside.

The 100-Mile City is a linear Barceloneta, a circular Rome, a stretched Porto. Suburbia reprogrammed, hybridised, compressed.

Ride the 100-Mile high-speed orbital monorail, a souped up Circle Line, where the loose ends and frayed edges of London's transport system – its isolated city-edge train and bus termini – are instantly, meaningfully, usefully connected with circus ride technology. Bexley to Brentford in 40 minutes: super-functional, super-fast and super-fun.

And, over time, watch our city grow inwards, spreading like wildfire through wasteful, anti-social, car-choked suburbia – eastwards from Richmond, west across the Newham Marshes, up from Eltham, across the hills of Greenwich and the empty golf courses of Enfield. Metroland back-filled, integrated, urbanised. London for 40 million people. A kind of inside-out Plan Voisin–Ville Radieuse, Blighty-style.

So rather than building out into the Green Belt, why not build inwards?

Gee's film takes this question and proceeds as a kind of lightly ironic, archaeological field trip into the past of the 100-Mile City. What was once there? What did prospective inhabitants want? What administrative and logistical problems had to be overcome? To investigate such questions, the filmmakers set out by bicycle on an epic journey along the site of the future city, circumnavigating London 15 miles out, just inside the Green Belt. Each mile along the way we filmed a single scene: 100 miles, 100 shots.

Film is combined with the voices of a wide range of people whose lives would be touched by the 100-Mile City: families presently unable to afford a home; developers and politicians who would design and administer the massive project; current residents of suburbia who're quite happy with the way things are; smallholders outlining the ways in which adjacent land would become a major new agricultural region;

lost tourists, bored teenagers, golfers, street ranters. Their voices combine and overlap to become a forum discussing the vision of the city, like a particularly lively episode of Question Time, but with better jokes.

As the film progresses along the route of the future city, and the contributors' voices begin to accumulate and give us a richer image of what, exactly, that city might be, the imagery of the film gets richer too. We get glimpses of our model of the 100-Mile City with images of the current suburban scene projected onto it. The filmmakers travel to other cities to film urban elements that inspired the original vision of the city: Porto, Barceloneta, Wuppertal (for the great monorail). Scenes of these good-city elements are spliced into the video of existing suburbia to produce a new space. The film becomes a collage city.

Stylistically, the film lies somewhere between Patrick Keiller's deadpan dissection of the British landscape in 'Robinson in Space' and DA Pennebaker's rollicking, visual-jazz montage 'Daybreak Express'. The soundtrack is joyful, stomping rhythm and blues: pounding out the miles.

100-Mile City, civic square

1_1.102.1

1_1.173.1

1_1.219.1

1_1.168.1

100-Mile City, video stills

The focus of all four of the projects described here is the design of a public or shared space that brings people into close proximity, making them highly visible to one another and therefore more likely to actually meet. These are projects intended to promote a high level of interdependence between individuals. In the long term, we also hope that they will help to empower strongly self-determined groups of people.

All of these projects are driven by a realistic yet profoundly optimistic view of society and of the role architecture can play in making our cities both socially and economically sustainable.

100-Mile City, model and detailed elevation

FARSHID MOUSSAVI

Born in Iran in 1965, Farshid Moussavi studied architecture at the University of Dundee; the Bartlett, University College London; and Harvard Graduate School of Design before working with the Office for Metropolitan Architecture. In 1993 she co-founded Foreign Office Architects, a practice thrust to global prominence two years later when it won the competition for the Yokohama International Port Terminal (2002). Subsequent projects included Carabanchel Housing, Madrid (2007), John Lewis Department Store and Cineplex in Leicester (2008), and Ravensbourne College, Greenwich (2010). Following the demerger of FOA in 2011, Moussavi established Farshid Moussavi Architecture (FMA). Completed projects of FMA include the Museum of Contemporary Art, Cleveland (2012) and two affordable housing projects in France, La Folie Divine, Montpellier and Îlot 19 La Défense-Nanterre, on the outskirts of Paris, both completed in 2017. Parallel to her professional practice, Moussavi is a prominent academic and writer. Since 2005 she has been Professor in Practice of Architecture at Harvard University Graduate School of Design, with which she has published three critically acclaimed books, *The Function of Ornament* (2006), *The Function of Form* (2009) and *The Function of Style* (2015). Moussavi was elected a Royal Academician in 2015. The talk took place at the Royal Geographical Society on 22 June 2017.

Photographs accompanying this text are by: FMA 84 (below), 115, 117 (left), 119 (below), 120 (above); Stephen Gill 86–87, 93, 100, 103, 104–105, 106–107, 109, 110–111; Google Maps 92; L'Image Contemporaine 100, 102 (right); Izumi Kobayashi 89 (below); Satoru Mishima 89 (above), 90; Paul Phung 116, 117 (right), 119 (above), 120 (below), 121 (above), 122, 124–125; Ramon Pratt 91; Frederik Soueix 102 (left); Mary Ann Sullivan 84 (above). The image on page 94 is a screenshot from *The Conversation*, 1974, directed by Francis Ford Coppola

Today we are constantly surrounded by politics with a capital P: big issues, grand narratives, large-scale changes. And as citizens we have become even more aware that we have a role to play, by exerting our agency as activists. But as architects, what is our role? How can we, as architects, make things different?

Like any other citizen, we can vote, march and sign petitions, all of which can be instrumental in influencing long-term strategies. We can also engage in a kind of professional activism by volunteering in the developing world, for instance, or taking an ethical stand on the countries or kinds of clients we will work for, or even fund-raising to build projects ourselves.

But what about buildings? I would like to talk about the politics of buildings, not in theory, but in practice. By this I mean the way buildings, in the absence of the architect, continually influence the micro-politics of everyday life.

In some of the best-known historical manifestos, we find buildings treated as a means to facilitate an ideal vision of how architecture should be connected to – and even change – the world. Think of Semper, who wanted all buildings to be made with motifs and patterns originating in fabrication techniques, as a way of generating symbolic meaning; or of Giedeon's notion that buildings had to express the spirit of an age. The modernists were clear that this spirit was made manifest in techniques of industrialisation and mass production.

However admirable such ideals, these manifestos focused more on the representation of external narratives than on the actual role buildings

play in our lives. Today, we need to consider a more direct way to insti-
gate a building's political potential. The process of design is inundated
by diverse requirements that relate to the politics of everyday life. Space
planning, security, rights-of-light, fire engineering, sustainability engineering, facade engineering, health and safety – each has an associated
consultant and enters the design process at different moments, intro-
ducing a large element of unpredictability. Enhanced levels of security
may require imminent changes to the entry sequence of a building early
on in the process, whereas new environmental regulations may neces-
sitate changes to the envelope design midway through. The election of
a new city mayor, usually every four years, may imply change in the space
programme, budget or even building location.

It is the task of the architect to coordinate these different coefficients
for buildings and their associated consultants and determine how they
interrelate. And it so happens that this same process suggests a means
of influencing the politics of buildings, or the relations between architecture and everyday life – not by bringing a building's elements into the
service of a grand narrative, but rather by arranging them in such a way
that they produce *affects*.

Affect, as used in the philosophy of Spinoza, and elaborated by
Bergson, Deleuze and Guattari, is pertinent to the discussion of architecture and politics. Transmitted by bodies, or objects such as buildings,
affects lead to the augmentation or diminution of a body's capacity
to act, as a result of how they are assembled.

And as they exist independent of, and prior to, people's interaction
with them, they are prior to language, and polysemic in nature. People
can interpret and respond to the affects they encounter in different ways,
according to their own unique sensibilities. Affects therefore play an
important role in defining the democratic and participatory relationship
between people and buildings.

A gate introduced within the perimeter wall of a building may generate affects of closure and traversability; handrails located around
museum exhibits may generate affects of visibility and untouchability;
or skylights in a train station may generate affects of transparency and
protection.

So what is the agency of the architect within this process of assem-
bling a building? Imagine that you're buying an apartment. You survey
its spaces and begin to occupy them in your mind. The placement of
a window in the bedroom is an architectural decision. If the architect
locates it centrally, the room might comply with environmental regulations, or the budget for the amount of glass, but it would be impossible
for you, the user, to locate your bed and have privacy. But if the architect

locates the window asymmetrically, the room continues to comply with regulations and the budget but it also provides privacy for the bed and illumination for an armchair to sit and read a book.

This approach locates the question of agency, not in what a building represents, but in the way it connects with people in their everyday life.

Here (right) is the east wing of the Smithsonian by I M Pei. Unlike the interior of the museum, where people are discouraged from touching the precious artefacts, the exterior is designed with blade-like corners whose affect of sharpness is so inviting to the touch that visitors have partly worn the edges away.

Similarly, at the Guggenheim Museum (below), the affect of lowness of the handrail invites visitors to recline. Rather than passing quickly through the ramping galleries as if they were supermarket aisles, people stop and lean on the handrails while they look at the art.

But what does thinking of buildings as aesthetic propositions mean for users? Do they have agency in this relationship? It is usual to discuss the relationship between objects and people in everyday life in terms of the agency of human subjects. The field of phenomenology, for instance, is concerned with how people gain access to the 'being' of objects – objects themselves are not usually considered to have agency. Of course, the difference between the objects discussed in philosophy and the architectural objects or buildings that people actually encounter is that buildings don't exist as ready-mades, but are arranged through the architectural process.

Here is a Cineplex in Leicester designed by my previous practice, FOA. The cluster of affects of reflectivity, glare and deformation transmitted by its mirror stainless steel rainscreen cladding means that the Cineplex is not ignored, as is often the case with such inward-looking buildings. On the contrary, at a couple of points around the perimeter, passersby of all ages stop and salute the building, systematically.

There is no reason why people should respect this building – it was certainly not part of our client's brief, nor was it a cultural response we hoped to evoke or a message that we, as the architects, wished to convey.

Rather, like the handrails which serve both to stop people falling into the Guggenheim atrium and to skew the conventions around the art encounter, or the walls which both shield the Smithsonian galleries from the elements and free people from the protective separateness that usually characterises the gallery encounter, the envelope of the Cineplex

is a consequence of the practical demand for dark interiors as well as the desire to generate affects that disrupt the habitual ways of engaging with this kind of building in the city.

What's going on here cannot be reduced to either the agency of the object or the subjectivity of the passerby: it is produced by them, together, or else arises through their encounter. The traditional representational approach to buildings assumes that there is a direct road from the act of looking at a building to the fact of understanding it. We now know this isn't true.

Recognising that the encounter between people and buildings is a co-production brings us closer to a non-anthropocentric conception of agency. For example, a residential building may transmit affects of flexibility, transparency and differentiation inside, and scalelessness and privacy outside. Some people may only experience the building as passersby, while others who live in it may encounter all of its affects, which result from the way its different elements have been styled or arranged. Through these encounters, people construct their own unique, experience-based knowledge of the world.

So, having discarded the idea that architecture can determine meanings for people – the same meanings for everyone simultaneously – we can now define the politics or agency of buildings in the following way:

The politics of buildings resides in their arrangement or assemblage. It manifests itself as a cluster of affects that spreads outwards from the building and influences the thoughts and activities of the people who engage with the building as they take part in everyday activities like residing or working. And because affects are non-deterministic, buildings are political without being deterministic: rather, they are propositions.

But how do these ambitions stand up to the realities of practice? The word agency implies that the architect has a certain freedom to arrange elements differently. Is this only possible with publicly funded projects? What about the commercial realities of practice, which tend to encourage repetition of the same?

Consider the interior of a cinema. When a certain way of arranging one of its elements – like its seats – is repeated over and over, this arrangement acquires a 'naturalness', so that it begins to be accepted unthinkingly, as the only way to watch a movie. Conversely, if the convention of seating arrangement is shifted, this generates a new cinema presence that loosens the traditional relationship between people and the activity of watching movies. Even if just for a brief moment, a sense of surprise or freedom opens up.

But what is the aim of shifting conventions? Why try to change the relationship between people and buildings?

The Yokohama Passenger Port Terminal was a project where we, as the architects, shifted a number of conventions that influence how people typically engage with a building for travelling. The dominant way of arranging a terminal is around a linear circulation route that moves passengers as directly as possible to the gates – and in the process reduces its experience to a thoroughfare. Instead, we designed a looped circulation system through bifurcating terminal floors with seamless connections to levels above and below. Freed from the habit of passively passing through, people might choose to use the terminal in different ways – as a place to sit down and paint, for example. By shifting these conventions, we generated a new ferry terminal assemblage that loosens the building's traditional relationship with travelling and allows people the freedom to respond to it creatively.

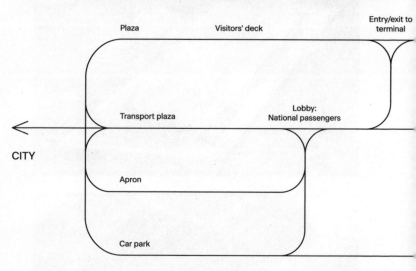

Plaza

Visitors' deck

Entry/exit to terminal

Transport plaza

Lobby:
National passengers

CITY

Apron

Car park

The philosopher Jacques Rancière argues that it is the distribution of the sensible – of what can be apprehended by the senses – that determines the possibilities for individuals to participate in daily life. For Rancière politics is a disruption, or 'dissensus', in conventionally perceived or prescribed spaces to *make that which did not possess grounds to be seen, seen*'. By disrupting the conventions of how everyday activities are arranged, architects open up possibilities to change the way the bodies

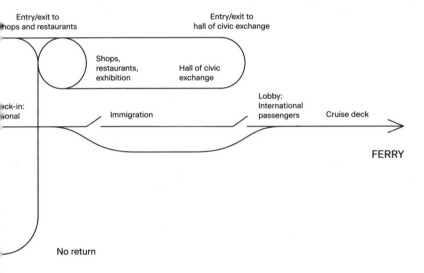

of individuals are supposed to fit those everyday activities. In so doing, they ground buildings in the micro-politics of everyday life.

I think the role of the architect is neither to communicate narratives nor to tell people the right or wrong way to use a terminal or watch movies or live in houses or work in offices. It is not deterministic, but rather resides in creating a 'dissensus' in how buildings are conventionally perceived, so that passive participation gives way to active encounters.

I am going to use two of our recent projects as a way to illustrate the impact of this approach on our design process.

The first one is a residential project that we recently completed for a site in Paris adjacent to the *Grande Axe*. It is the first residential building to have been built in La Défense, the major business district west of the city, in 30 years. It is also the result of a unique way in which private developments are procured in France, led by the council, with a focus on design. We were selected by a local developer, alongside two other architectural practices, to be part of their bid for the site. Our client's bid was chosen by EPADESA, the development office in charge of the masterplan for the area, partly because of their financial proposal and partly because of the design value they promised to bring to the project. We then had to compete with the other two architectural practices in our client's bid and present in front of the mayor, who personally chose our scheme. Post-competition, EPADESA oversaw our design development on behalf of the mayor to ensure that the competition proposal was not diluted along the way.

I think this way of procuring housing in France is interesting because it allows the local authority to decide on the mix of housing developed on each site, and the design, without having to deliver themselves. Also, by dividing the work between different developers, the city becomes more diverse and the housing stock less formulaic.

The site and the question of housing suggested a number of conventions which we chose to challenge.

First, *the strict separation between public and private in the urban context, or the way that living in the city limits people's interaction with the outdoors.*

Our site sits sandwiched between two cemeteries at the moment of transition between the historic *Axe* and its extension towards the River Seine. This exceptional location left it poised for a new type of relationship, not only with the *Axe*, but also with the natural environment.

In a multi-storey residential building, the envelope is the agent determining the relationship between public and private, inside and outside, and the way the building is integrated into its context. The shape of the envelope, as dictated by the site outline and the area masterplan, would be a deep wedge-like slab perpetuating the conventional divide between inside and out along the *Axe*. Even if the envelope were designed with balconies, which provide an in-between zone, balcony divisions usually limit interaction between inside and out – sometimes you have to twist out of the balcony to see the urban space just outside.

The second convention we considered was the way that *living in the city forces people to choose between communal life and segregation*. The floor plates of residential buildings, owing to their length and depth, are the agent determining the size and number of units on any one floor. A deep slab would lead to a long, artificially lit central circulation corridor flanked either side by dark and stuffy single-aspect apartments.

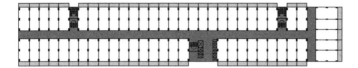

Le Corbusier, Unité d'habitation

Mies van der Rohe, Lafayette Park

The communal corridor is a vestige of the modernist vision of communal housing, which went so far as to propose that not only hallways but also bathrooms, kitchens, dining rooms, terraces and even telephones were shared – a model of coexistence dating from a time of much greater social homogeneity, dominated by the nuclear family. Today, a household may equally well comprise singles, divorcees, same-sex families, co-living, multi-generations, the elderly. These diverse living arrangements imply very different habits and desires. Neighbours no longer leave for work and return home at similar times of day. Instead, you have unpredictable and disruptive comings and goings and, increasingly, the experience of living among a rotation of strangers, thanks to the rise of Airbnb.

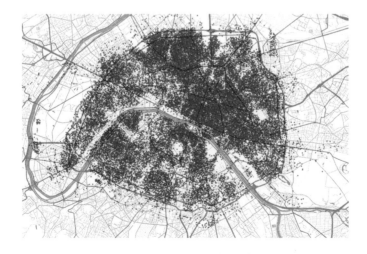

'Inside Airbnb' data project showing 61,152 listings in Paris

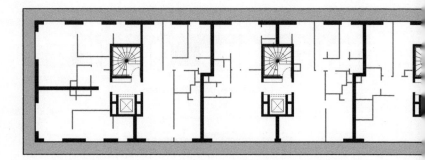

So designing for such buildings should begin from understanding the fact that people live in close proximity, in a single building, *not* because they want to sustain a communal life, but rather because there isn't enough space in the city for everyone to have their own house.

An alternative approach to communal housing has been to design different kinds of residential buildings to suit different household types. The 'Collective Old Oak' in London is an example of a 'co-living' building for single young professionals. It provides private bedrooms, a little like a hotel, and communal cooking, eating and living areas for socialising and networking. Or there are Germany's 'Multigeneration Houses', which bring together a kindergarten, a social centre for the elderly and a drop in centre for young families in an attempt to simultaneously tackle the social isolation of the elderly population and the rising cost of childcare.

But is segregating different types of households the right answer? For a start, specialised housing means that people have to move when

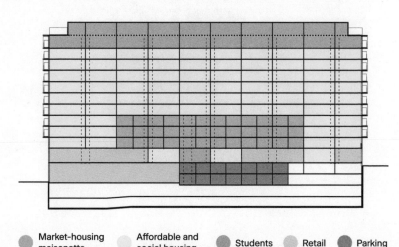

● Market-housing maisonette   ● Affordable and social housing   ● Students   ● Retail   ● Parking

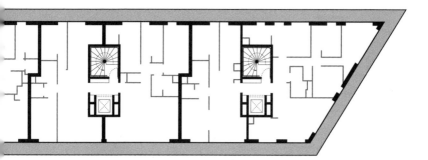

their status changes. It also promotes a kind of ghettoisation, with young professionals concentrated in the periphery of the city, and wealthy families in the city centre. Moreover, the emphasis tends to be on 'affordable' housing, which in architectural terms usually translates into stripped back aesthetics designed to promote the most expedient delivery possible.

Can we not instead find a solution for living in the city together, but *separately*? The brief outlined by Nanterre's communist mayor was radical, asking that we accommodate different household types in one building: 91 social and price-capped apartment units, 110 rooms for students and one level of maisonette penthouses. Rather than the segregation approach or forced communal model, we saw our agency as generating a new model that allows residents both to live in privacy within their multi-storey building and to live closer to the exterior natural environment.

To achieve this, the building is arranged as an assemblage of elements that by virtue of their location and grouping could perform in the following ways:

To avoid the typical corridor arrangement that forces sociability and collectivity on the residents, the envelope does not occupy the full depth of the site, but instead forms a shallow 12m slab. The slab is divided laterally into pairs of apartments, each sharing a lift and stair around a small landing. As the corridor is eliminated altogether, this generates an unusual degree of privacy for the residents, enabling different types of households to occupy the same building.

The cores, party walls between apartments, and walls along the exterior envelope are mobilised as a group to act as the building's load-bearing structure. Since there are no fixed walls in the interiors, residents have the power to reconfigure their apartment over time – or even before they move in. All apartment interiors, regardless of their tenure type, are furnished only with very basic interior fixtures and fittings, so that each resident can finish them according to their personal preferences and resources.

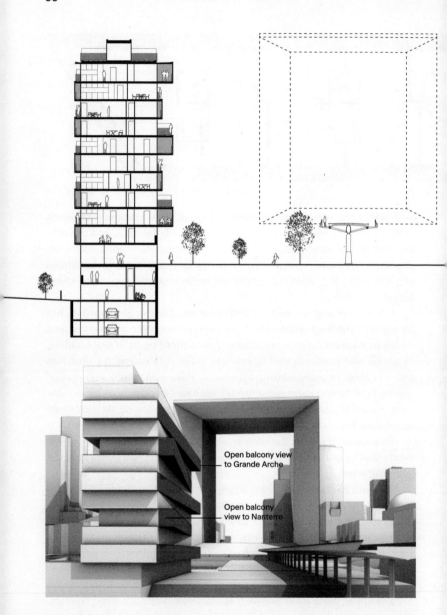

Open balcony view
to Grande Arche

Open balcony
view to Nanterre

As the units are dual-aspect, they can be fully glazed at both ends, to benefit from an abundant supply of natural ventilation. To shift the strict separation between the building and the exterior open space defined by the *Grande Axe*, each floor plate is tapered by two degrees in alternate orientations, so that the building transmits axiality instead of verticality.

The tapered shape of the floor plates not only integrates the building with the *Axe*, but carries an environmental agency too. It generates a stepped silhouette on the south, east and west sides of the building, as a consequence of which only the protruding floors require shutters for shade and privacy.

The exterior envelope is designed to reinforce the sense of inclusivity. All the elements common to the different residents are designed in the same way (marked here in colour). This is something like the unified envelope that wraps the typical Haussmann urban block, absorbing people's different paths in life and distinct economic statuses, with the understanding that in the end the city belongs to all, not only to the rich. Except that a Haussmann block is based on the repetition of standard types of apartments that vary only in ceiling height, and it provides no exterior space.

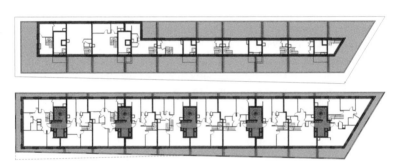

Market-housing maisonette, upper and lower floors

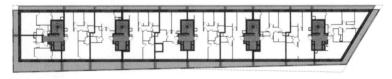

Affordable housing

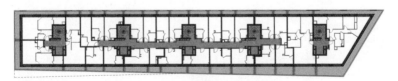

Student and social housing

 Envelope   Balcony divisions   Open space   Circulation

In our case, the stepped silhouette differentiates the outdoor spaces of each apartment into a recessed balcony on one side, and a protruding loggia on the other. These act as intermediate spaces, neither completely closed nor completely open, and as their orientation and size vary from floor to floor, as well as along the building length, owing to the scissoring of the floors, an unusual level of diversity of apartments is generated behind the unified envelope. The size of exterior space, or contact with nature, is therefore the defining feature that differentiates one apartment from the other.

You can see from the plans that the penthouse apartments are not really much bigger than the standard social housing units; they just have larger terraces. The balconies and loggias themselves are assembled from smaller elements: shutters, handrails, dividing walls, soffits and glazed walls. Tectonic and material decisions regarding each one of these sub-elements or micro-agents were guided, *not* by any preconceptions of what an affordable residential building should look like, but rather by a concern with durability and low maintenance, and a desire to enhance the residents' relationship to the exterior. Moreover, these outdoor spaces are assembled, not as a thin membrane that simply protects each unit from the elements in a fixed way, but as a zone that residents can appropriate in different ways over time.

The anodised aluminium shutters of the loggias are designed with diamond-shaped extrusions to maximise their transparency towards oblique views – of the *Axe* and the wide-open space around it – while

minimising their transparency along frontal views. As the depth of the loggias varies along the length of the building, the shutters appear with different levels of transparency and change shade as they catch the light. Shifting from light grey to dark blue-grey and blue-black in the course of the same day, they imbue the building with an affect of temporality and make the passerby aware of the passage of time.

The shutters are designed to slide, giving residents the option to enclose the loggias entirely, or leave them partially open to frame a view, or slide them to one side to transform the loggia into an open balcony. Another element of the loggias is the dividing walls between neighbours, designed in mirror-backed glass to bring a sense of expansiveness into the loggia – as if there were no walls there at all. The reflective glass also displaces the distant natural scene, bringing it forward so that it appears part of the built foreground.

The visual connection to a recognisable feature of the urban land-scape not only gives the resident an unmistakable sense of where they are, but also makes them feel their home belongs to this specific context. Moreover, the unique views reflected within each loggia create a building in which no two apartments have the same experience.

The other wall in the loggia – the one that divides it from the interior – is 50 per cent solid and 50 per cent glazed, partly for structural reasons and partly to obtain the necessary U-values for the interiors.

As the solid areas stack from floor to floor, they would ordinarily superimpose verticality on the axiality of the floors. To suppress this verticality, the solid walls are clad with mirror-backed glass, generating a strong affect of axiality as well as temporality since reflections on them change throughout the day. Along each loggia, the experience of solidity is therefore exchanged for liquidity, lightness or delicacy.

In contrast to the intimacy of loggias, the assemblage of the balconies establishes a greater continuity between each household and the exterior, which ranges in scale as the height of the balconies varies with the stepped silhouette of the building. As they are naturally shaded by the floors above, the balconies are left as open verandas. The soffits are painted a very dark grey, to frame the exterior landscape and reduce the visual presence of the expansion joints of its concrete slab.

As in the loggias, the dividing walls of the balconies are made of glass. The reflective walls 'borrow scenery' from the distant landscape and obscure the spatial depth clues which normally indicate the true distance

from the exterior landscape. Therefore, although clearly a 'built' space, the balcony creates the illusion of continuity with nature. What is behind is projected forward, merging with the foreground, creating a new land-scape which only exists in relation to the unique standpoint from which each resident occupies the balcony.

The building and exterior space are therefore continually becoming one, an ambiguous space created by blurred boundaries.

The handrail is another agent that defines the experience of each balcony. It is fully glazed with no metal supports, frit in a graduated pat-tern from the floor up, simply to indicate its presence and give a low-level privacy where furniture may be located, but fading away to allow light to reach plants kept on the balconies.

Residents' belongings were moved in recently, via tall ladders resting on the facade, apparently not an unusual occurrence in France! And in itself quite a spectacle.

Already in the first week, it was obvious that the residents are of all kinds and backgrounds, and that even the process of the move meant different things to them.

Could this be a single man occupying the corner apartment that faces the sports arena? And here is a small family focusing on the move... Here a more traditional household with a grandmother living with the family. The first thing they did was furnish the balcony so they could convene for meals. Here a student.

And an astonishing number of residents, even in their first week, chose to work on their gardens.

It has been telling that these different households, rather than choosing to have a residents' association that meets in person, have opted to start a Facebook group to communicate among themselves. A few of them have posted photos of their apartment to me. Like Jean Pierre fitting out his interior to his own specifications – we see natural light flooding into his apartment.

I think the building is one that allows people with very different lives to live side by side without disturbing each other. In that sense it is very private, but also extremely urban. Standing on the balcony of the apartment, you can look all the way through to the loggia at the other end. Wherever you are, there is a great sense of continuity between interior and exterior.

If a building is a proposition, rather than a determination, then of course the only way to judge how a building's assemblage really influences people in their everyday lives is retrospectively, when people are actually using it.

Working with the photographer Stephen Gill, I have tried to document the ongoing relationships unfolding between the building and its users and its context. Already in the first week, life was pouring out of the interiors into the loggias and balconies, with people using their exterior spaces in all kinds of ways.

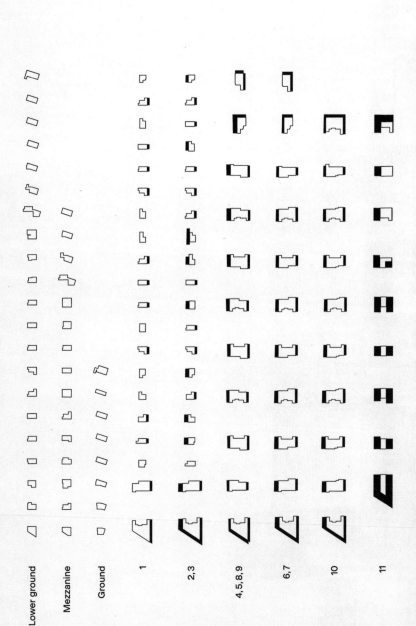

But it is not only the engagement of residents that animates the building. The building also changes in relation to light and colour during the course of the day, from mid-morning, to late afternoon, to early evening, when it becomes quite dark, even brittle-looking. When the sky is blue, the building captures it all over. From a distance, the blue unifies the different floors and the building gains a sense of liquidity. When the sky is grey, the building appears more grey too.

The building's appearance also changes depending on where a person is in relation to it. From the cemetery, it looks flat, as the loggias and balconies are aligned, whereas along the south facade, facing the *Axe*, the building transmits axiality. Seen up close, the shutters reveal their sheer thinness, while the handrail of the balconies captures the blue sky and appears opaque. From another angle, the handrails become semi-transparent and seem to dissolve into the reflective balcony divisions, glazed and solid walls, so that the various elements are hard to tell apart.

From wherever you stand, it is also impossible to see where the students live, or where the smaller or larger apartments are, just like in a Haussmann block. Rather than expressing the variability of inhabitants' incomes, the building's elements are arranged to express variability in a more inclusive way, through the changing environment, different points of view, changing uses of outdoor space, the flux of time and weather. Seen from below it transmits floating, stacking and shearing, like a building on the move.

If there is a politics in this building, then it is of a different kind – a kind that can only be done by the building. It relies not on a high budget, but on the use of ordinary elements, assembled in a way that challenges preconceptions about what modern housing should look like, and how we should live. We saw our task as architects to engage these architectural elements to promote equality, both aesthetically, by creating a building which appears equally crafted across all levels of affordability, and practically, by providing similar levels of privacy, light, fresh air and flexibility across the different apartment types, rejecting the notion that these are luxuries which only the privileged few are entitled to.

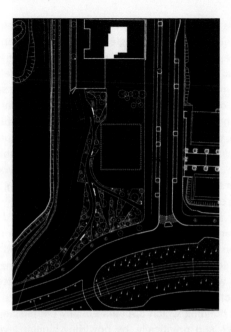

Next, then, I would like to share with you another housing project for the City of Montpellier in the south of France with a fairly modest budget of 3.8 million euros. It is smaller than Nanterre, housing just 36 apartments, but it follows the same procurement strategy I mentioned previously.

Given their similar use, many of our aims for the building were the same, namely: subverting the assumption that affordable housing must be synonymous with uniformity, maximising flexibility for residents, minimising communal circulation spaces and providing ample private exterior spaces.

But the brief, set out by the City of Montpellier, posed an additional question: how to design this residential building as the first of 12 'follies' they planned as a continuation of a history of folly-building dating back to the eighteenth century. In the French and English tradition, the folly was a playful structure carefully placed within a garden or landscape to reflect the values of travel, learning, pleasure and luxury. So the folly was about a leap beyond the practical. However, we understood that by setting the folly as the brief for housing the City of Montpellier was asking *how can we push the idea of housing beyond its usual reasoning* – how can the folly's playfulness be used as a critical tool to generate a new possibility for housing?

Given Montpellier's warm climate, we decided to use the idea of the folly in the garden to generate a building that promoted indoor–outdoor living. As at Nanterre, the building is arranged as an assemblage of elements. The core, structure and services together act as one agent, the floor plates, handrails and envelope together act as another agent, and this is how they perform:

The envelope is designed as a compact nine-storey shape, the maximum height permitted by the masterplan for the area. The compactness of the building leaves space for a garden all around, and maximises distant views for all the apartments. The concrete core and service risers are located centrally, with concrete load-bearing walls along the perimeter. Freeing the apartments of fixed elements allows residents to reconfigure their interior layouts as needed – as at Nanterre.

Insetting the external envelope generates balconies all around, while the remainder of the floor plate, owing to its small size, is subdivided into four corner residential units, with cross-ventilation. A surround balcony would require dividing screens between neighbours, limiting lateral views. If the balconies are pinched at the border between apartments, these screens are not needed, but a clear divide continues to exist between the interior and the balconies. Our idea of promoting indoor–outdoor living required us to approach the building envelope differently – not as a strict divide between inside and outside, but as a border that is constantly shifting in response to the many inflections of the envelope.

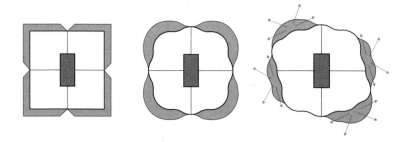

To achieve this, the envelope of the corner apartments was first curved with three points of inflection, and the balconies with one point of inflection. The corner balconies flowed better around the corner; however, in this scenario, neighbouring balconies still overlooked each other laterally. They presented overlooking vertically too, since the balconies are simply stacked on top of one another. The envelope curvature of each apartment was then changed from three points of inflection to five, while the curvature of two of the balconies was also changed from one point of inflection to three. With this new geometry, balconies have 180-degree views out but they don't overlook each other, while the increased number of inflections in the envelope continually grows the interior or the exterior along the length of each apartment, presenting an experience of constant openness or anticipation towards the outdoors.

In order to reduce the overlooking of balconies vertically, the inflections in the envelope and the balcony edge profile are varied further, to produce two different types of floor shapes, and these are then rotated and mirrored around the axis of the core to generate four different typical floor configurations.

The five apartment types required by the client's brief, based on size, are therefore diversified by being given different shapes, different orientations and balconies of varying size and form. To shift the building arrangement even further from uniformity, these four typical floors are used twice along the height of the building in an alternating order. As a result, each of the 36 apartments is of a different kind, amplifying the choice provided to prospective residents.

As at Nanterre, residents who put down a deposit to buy an apartment are able to modify its internal divisions. It has been interesting to watch how they decide to divide their space, creating rooms that are ever-uniquely shaped, thanks to the inflections in the envelope.

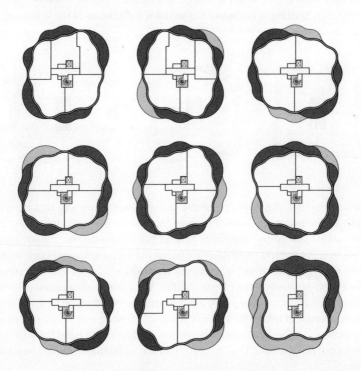

As a consequence of the alternate stacking of the four typical floors, the positions of the balconies also shift from one floor to another, generating the impression that the floor plates are randomly changing, as if the building's shape were merely the result of foolish playfulness – like a folly!

Except this 'apparent randomness' provides the building with a stepped silhouette and generates two types of balconies – single-height and double-height – as at Nanterre, with the difference that here they are two floors away from the balcony above or below, meaning they are less exposed to the neighbours' gaze. To minimise downward over-looking even further, the handrails of some balconies have to generate a gradient of privacy along their length. In a residential building, the handrail typically performs two contradictory roles: to allow maximum views out of each balcony, and minimum views in from the exterior. In our case it has a third task of minimising views to the balconies two floors below.

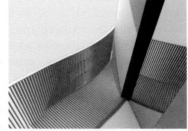

The profile chosen for the handrail supports and its distribution can play a significant role in performing these roles. Having looked at different options, we chose two rows of circular profiles offset with one another. This creates a moiré effect when viewed obliquely, which is how it will be seen all the time from the exterior, given the constant inflections in the shape of the building. The moiré effect reduces views in, while maintaining views out.

To minimise vertical overlooking, the spacing of the supports is densified. In line with the preferred practice in France, load-bearing walls, floor slabs and the core are constructed in concrete, which has to be insulated and clad. Our low budget ruled out the use of different bespoke curved cladding panels. To minimise the faceting of the curves, then, the structural walls along the perimeter are clad in corrugated anodised aluminium panels, which can be bent easily, and disguise the seams in the recesses of the corrugated profile. They also require no maintenance and avoid glare for passersby, as the corrugation breaks up reflections.

Instead of one type of corrugated panel, however, three different scales are used: the smallest or tightest is applied to the convex areas, and the largest to the concave areas. To emphasise the curvature of the envelope through shadows, the glazing, which could not be curved either, is inset and modulated to approximate the curvature of the envelope.

Since this project is not yet complete, we have not been able to see for ourselves how its arrangement forms different relationships with the people who live in it and encounter it. We can only imagine how the choice of a single-height, extremely private balcony, with an exterior curtain for additional privacy, will provoke different responses from the double-height balconies.

Nor do we know how the different sizes, shapes and orientations of rooms will be experienced by the people who occupy them. We can however imagine that a curvilinear envelope with many different orientations, bringing different views to each of the apartments, will be experienced in an entirely different way from an orthogonal envelope that provides a maximum of two orientations.

The unique location and orientation of each balcony will frame the exterior differently for residents, so no two balcony views will be identical. And the curvilinear shape of the balcony will bring different amounts of shade to each resident; sitting under it will be similar, perhaps, to sitting under a tree, sometimes a smaller tree, sometimes a larger one, but always in extreme privacy. Together with the indoor–outdoor continuity of each apartment and the mild climate of Montpellier, this is bound to prompt its residents to use their balconies in unexpected ways.

So the building's politics, like those of the Nanterre project, work at a micro-level, arranging its elements in a peculiar way to open up new possibilities for those who would use it, like a folly in a park.

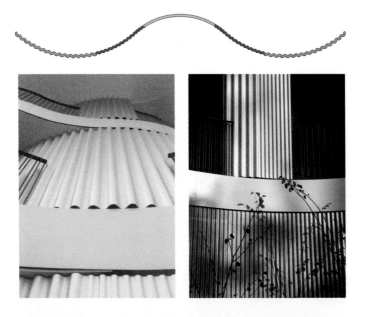

116

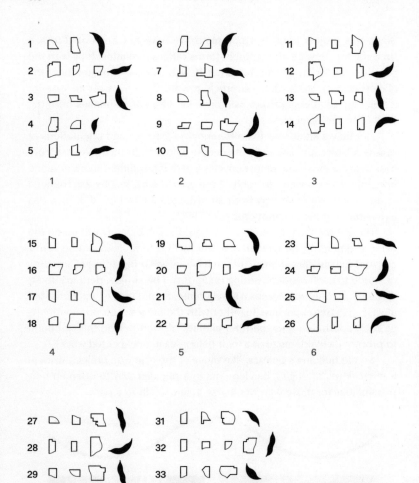

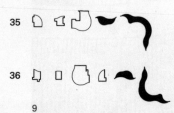

Just to end on a more general level. I have been trying to show that approaching buildings as an assemblage is a relevant way of working today, not least because it has political objectives. This politics is different from a political statement: both because a building is not the same as the words we use to describe it, and because a building is political if its specific elements and arrangement cause its users to change how they see it and respond to it in their thoughts and actions. This liberating process can happen in small ways, but cumulatively these can become a powerful political tool – and one that I think is more effective than the architectural manifesto with its holistic political aims, which do not correspond to the way buildings are actually experienced and perceived.

A building as an assemblage cannot be grasped as a whole object at once, as you can see at a very prosaic level through the different experiences that the buildings in Nanterre and Montpellier offer. I have been showing these buildings at a micro-level, element by element, because that is how these buildings are experienced – at a micro-level.

The complexity of the entire design process makes it impossible to stick to a simple objective – buildings end up differently from the words or images we use to describe them when we start out. The realities of current practice are summed up very well in an email I received this morning from a former student, who now runs his own firm. He writes:

'The extension of a Fisac building in Andorra to convert it into a gallery got stopped the day we started on site, because of sudden financial turmoil on the client's side. The other one in Barcelona, politicians got involved, and decided to halt it too. But we will persist!

What now keeps us busy is a large skiable bridge in Andorra. It's a polemical project that parliament got involved in and there are hearings this week in parliamentary committees to see whether the permission we got from the government to go ahead is legal or not. Big mess. The project is in the news every day, bad kind of news because it's been politicised.'

I lately have the sense of being in a continuous and unending battle against regulations, bureaucrats, politicians, media, citizens, ecologists and an ever-expanding list of interest groups. And yet here we are, crystalline and innocent as ever, trying to convince them all with an endless production of arguments. It's tiring but it's fun.

At times when we wonder if and how our work is relevant anymore, I think it is important to remind ourselves that buildings can have an improving impact on people – not by telling them to do things differently but simply by letting them experience things differently – experience buildings, their place in buildings and, by extension, their place in society.

WITHERFORD WATSON
MANN ARCHITECTS

Having met as students at the University of Cambridge, Stephen Witherford (b 1967), Christopher Watson (b 1966) and William Mann (b 1966) collaborated on a series of entries in the Europan housing competition programme before formalising their practice in 2001. Their first substantial commission was to convert two former industrial buildings in Shoreditch into the headquarters of Amnesty International UK (2003–05). This project demonstrated a talent for the reuse of existing fabric which the architects would later apply to the expansion of the Whitechapel Art Gallery (2003–09), designed with Robbrecht en Daem Architecten, and the Stirling Prize-winning transformation of the ruins of Astley Castle near Nuneaton for the Landmark Trust (2007–12). In addition to three Europan wins (1999, 2001, 2005), the practice's work in the field of housing includes a group of 13 social housing apartments in Gistel, Belgium (2003–15), a block housing 27 apartments in northwest Cambridge (2012–17), and a contemporary almshouse in Bermondsey comprising 57 extra-care apartments with communal and public facilities (2014–). The talk took place at the Royal Geographical Society on 13 July 2017.

Photographs accompanying this text are by: Kristien Daem 128, 141–143; Philipp Ebeling 154, 156, 162; David Grandorge 131, 134, 139, 147–149, 151–152, 158; Witherford Watson Mann Architects 130, 136, 144, 145

HOUSING IS FIRST OF ALL A WORK OF IMAGINING THE CITY

Finishing two housing projects in the last two years has prompted us to reflect on the challenges of shared housing. It's just one strand of our work, but it's the one we chose to start our collaboration with. So, we've been trying to recall how things were, and what we were thinking when we started our work together 20 years ago. It's striking to see how the discourse in London around housing has changed almost beyond recognition in that time. By contrast, the way that our studio has been exploring and making housing has remained stubbornly consistent. That may not necessarily be a virtue – but it's only really with the completion of Gistel and Cambridge that the feedback loop closes and we can take stock.

We chose to focus on housing, initially, because we were interested in cities, particularly in how their design can support small-scale self-organisation. Our excitement about designing within the discipline of the city, and our ambivalence about the conditions we were working in, are expressed in a text we wrote part-way through this journey:

'Housing: this innocent participle, this -ing, carries a huge burden that makes designing housing almost unrecognisably different from designing houses. For housing, design is codified, construction industrialised and management institutionalised. But it is also an exhilarating intermediate scale between the comforts and tensions of the individual home and the bewildering, liberating extent of the city. Like Zola, Breughel, Antonioni, we move from empathy with the individual to the grand, untidy spectacle of the city, focusing on the scenes of encounter in between. Housing is first of all a work of imagining the city.'

We started our collaboration with a series of walks through the edges of London, driven by curiosity about our adoptive city. From the Lea Valley to the Westway, we encountered a city that was patchy, socially mixed, characterised in places by activism – for maintaining open space, allotments, local markets and housing. It was a porous, leaky city where awkward and vacated places gave rise to improvisation and non-prescribed activities.

We observed a city in a state of constant change. Some of those changes now feel familiar, but other practices seem so distant that it's hard to imagine we're talking about the recent past. Post-war social housing was being destroyed, slabs and towers were being replaced with houses – for example, at the Trowbridge Estate in Hackney. Victorian houses were still being removed to create Mile End Park; envisaged in Abercrombie's 1943 County of London Plan, it was only finished at the Millennium. And yet the population of the city was starting to grow. At first the new apartments and houses were built behind dock walls, in enclaves away from the shared city of schools, doctors and shops; then they spread along the canals, behind their protective moat.

When Martorell Bohigas Mackay from Barcelona were hired to pre-pare an urban plan for the Lea Valley in 1999, it was a sign of a new political climate in relation to cities. Their plan articulated an aspiration that London might embrace a more European approach, with the newly established mayor and the boroughs taking a close interest in the quality of public space, in urban rather than suburban densities, and in the role of public buildings in the city. That proposition seemed plausible at the time, but it's not quite how things have turned out.

Back then Europan offered young architects in Britain the opportunity to think about cities through the design of housing. It offered quite a discursive environment, with essays exploring challenges and approaches from across Europe. The briefs for sites were not prescriptive but were open to interpretation, responding to broader themes – it felt serious, necessary and relevant. In 1999 the theme was 'In-Between Cities' and the focus was on disused urban land; one of the three UK sites was in Peckham, south London.

We were committed to establishing an understanding of the city as a means to underpin our architectural thinking, and Europan was a way for us to start exploring this path.

In north Peckham we encountered a clash of approaches to housing. 1960s slab blocks lined the edge of Burgess Park like fortifications. The park was another creation of Abercrombie's plan for post-war London, and to make it a vast area of nineteenth-century terraces had been removed. Further south, the 1960s estates gave way to the 1990s estate-renewal programme, where two-storey terrace houses lined streets planted with saplings. Caught between these two models were the emerging ideas for new public spaces: the town square at the head of the old canal, a swimming pool, a new kind of multimedia public library and a performance platform 'gateway' thing. To the south, Peckham Road and the streets lined by Victorian terraces were largely intact.

The Europan site was to the west of the new square, behind the swimming pool and at the termination of a proposed new tram linking central and south London. It was wonderfully fragmented, with very different sorts of edges and an awkward shape defined by the curve of the high street being met by a small closed-off road. There was a last tooth of a nineteenth-century terrace, a new Wetherspoons pub, a Victorian school building now used for small businesses and workshops, and the large, blank new pool.

Our proposal began as perimeter block but became more broken and porous, pushing out and easing back to respond to the grain of the high street, school and square. The contortions of the buildings structured three new public spaces: two external rooms and one internal one. Residents' allotments created an active and sociable 'garden' at the heart of the proposal, a five-a-side football/basketball court provided a more combative arena, and an indoor sports centre doubled up as a local performance space.

The whole site was traversed north to south by two pathways. The heart of the urban block was a porous interior where young and old could express themselves and come together.

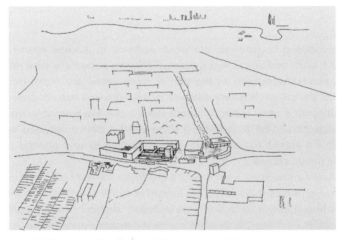

We proposed a generous enclosed walkway to access apartments on the east- and south-facing sides. This was potentially contentious, as walkways were seen as the root of many social problems. But our idea of the gallery was very different to the walkways that stretched for hundreds of metres linking different slab blocks. We wanted to make a place that could be occupied and shared, rather than empty and threatening – a glazed balcony overlooking the gardens and planted roofs of the public spaces.

And we imagined what it would be like to live here each day, close to the high street stalls selling Caribbean fruit. We saw that there were a lot of hospitals not far away, so we included 'shared houses' for groups of doctors or nurses, with guest rooms for families and friends. A new job description, 'key-worker', had tentatively entered the collective consciousness: it revealed the lurch from a city with affordable rents and homes to the speculative global city – although we did not understand this at the time.

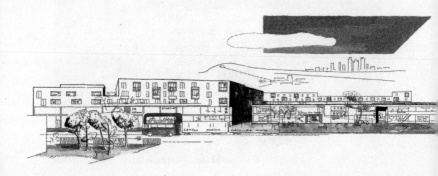

As we described it, Peckham '...has a feel of uncertainty but also of possibility... We wanted to catch this mix of openness and definition to make a piece of city where neither spaces nor objects dominate but where diverse situations – a sports hall, civic rooms, a nursery; flats, cafes and offices; allotments, winter gardens, a tram stop – sit side by side, where boundaries are loosely enough drawn to encourage appropriation but are still clear enough to deter abuse.'

Our early explorations of shared housing were indifferent to object-buildings, responding instead to the complex accumulations and erosions of place. The apartments were not mechanically repeated types, but flexed to shape diverse edges and social spaces. Together with the drawings and models we developed to explore our thinking – the interior views, the stretched elevations, the model representing the grain of individual apartments and collective, outdoor rooms – this experience provided us with most of the tools we would be using for the next 20 years.

We took part in Europan as a way to engage with a culture of city-making, one that seemed deeper-rooted in Amsterdam, Berlin or Basel than it was in London. Our connection to Flanders and Belgium was more unintentional; it followed fairly naturally from William's time working in Ghent and living in Brussels. But our exposure was no less deep or direct for its slightly accidental nature.

What we found was a fractured and dispersed urban environment: the cities were peppered with vacant sites – even quite centrally – and the fine mist of villages was spreading, slowly eroding the patchwork landscape of smallholdings. In Ghent and Brussels, we observed conventional architectural types sitting in unpredictable configurations. We saw how the city blocks had metamorphosed over centuries, their edges hardening and softening, their connections to interior yards filling and emptying. You see this particularly in the intimate streets of the Prinsenhof in Ghent, where Marie-Jose van Hee has built several houses of calm, luminous, slightly austere generosity.

It was also clear that the institutional framework was evolving. In the Flemish Region, the Spatial Structure Plan (*Ruimtelijk Structuurplan*) of 1997 looked to concentrate development in existing settlements. The introduction a year later of a government architect, the *Vlaams Bouwmeester*, created a new instrument for public procurement of architects, in the form of the Open Oproep, which matched skills to projects through a process that was light on paperwork and focused on design strategy. So, in terms of the emerging policy context, things were moving in a similar direction to London, superficially at least.

It was through the Open Oproep process that we were selected for a housing project in Gistel. We were tasked with building 13 apartments for older people, forming a new public space and restoring a seventeenth-century inn. The project was a collaboration between three clients: the Woonwel housing association, the town council and the regional ministry of public works. Located on a backyard site in the centre of a small town, this is the kind of project that only came about because the supply of land outside of settlements was severely limited by the Spatial Structure Plan. The low inn with its steep pantiled roof echoes the farms of the surrounding land, giving a sense of the rural landscape caught up by the rising tide of settlement growth.

You feel Gistel's early medieval morphology, with narrow terrace plots lining the old coastal road that winds through the town, and the lane that veers off to the west, terminating in the abbey in the marshes. The twists of these two roads create an unusually deep urban block, 200m by 120m, with the inn at its northeast corner. The site was bordered on two sides by streets and backed onto the rear gardens of neighbouring plots.

Our strategy was to pull the new housing to the back edge of the site, forming a new courtyard with the inn. This courtyard would be a shared garden for residents and a cafe terrace, enclosed by the interlocking Ls of the inn and the new housing, but at the same time porous to the surrounding streets. This required the housing to be built in a strip about 12m from the boundary, which obviously meant very compact planning, with small patio gardens. At the southeast corner, this had to taper to accommodate the stable wing of the inn, and we proposed a small passage here.

The scale of the courtyard followed clues from the site. The housing would be two storeys, similar in height to the roof ridge of the inn. The front doors of the ground-floor apartments would line the courtyard, while the first floor would be cut open by an access gallery and perforated

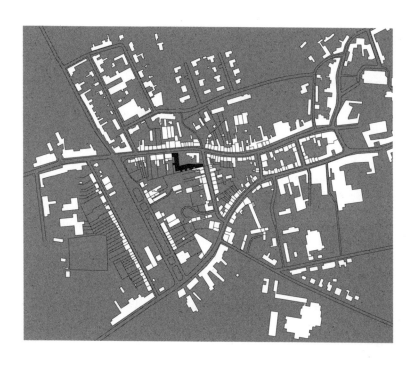

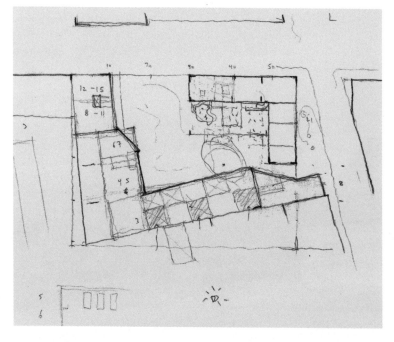

by roof terraces. Our landscape architect, Paul Deroose, designed a floor of purply clay pavers and a rectangle of grass, like a courtyard farm. Not without intent, the whole thing took on something of the character of the workers' housing they call *beluiken* in Ghent – a slice of urbanised countryside, intimate and very direct.

Our idea was deceptively simple: to draw the street into the depth of the site, excavating a pocket of collective space from this deep block. Yet, as our model shows, within the grain of narrow house plots lining the street, both this open space and the apartments alongside it are slightly alien. They add something different, not more of the same. Because they are shallow, the apartments present their broad face to the courtyard, the rhythms and proportions are more horizontal, and of course they repeat rather than being individual and different as all the houses are. In a country where social housing forms only five per cent of the housing stock, and where major public spaces are lined with narrow guildhouses jostling one another, this collective scale is quite unusual – even at this modest size.

And if our idea was simple, its realisation would be anything but.

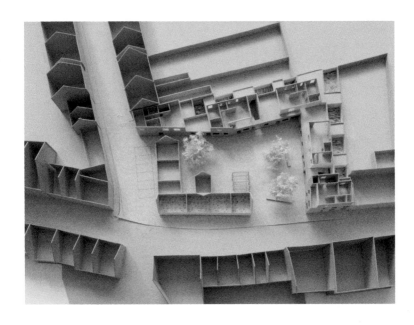

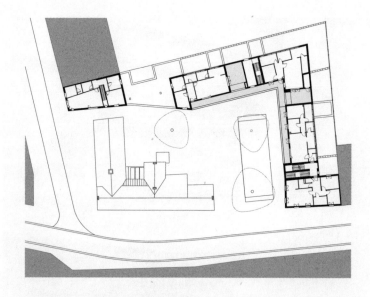

There are two main apartment types, both two-bed. On the ground floor we used L-shaped units, two and three rooms deep, so they are about 9m wide by 11m deep. We adjusted these to the geometry and orientation, squeezing the block to form a passage by the inn, where we put the cycle store and re-sited an electrical sub-station. These ground-floor flats face out to the edge of the site, offering a degree of privacy from the public courtyard, and the living room is lit by a patio.

Where the lower flats face the rear, those on the first floor could open up to the courtyard. These upper flats are accessed off two stairs and a short gallery. They are little more than 6m deep by 13m long, and their living rooms are parallel to the courtyard, lit on their long side; the three flats around the court have small patio roof terraces. The building heights vary to respond to existing conditions, stepping up to three storeys on the main street, and cutting down to a single storey by the café terrace.

The distortions of the site, together with the unbroken external and internal corners – one of the hardest challenges in designing housing – produce 13 one-off apartments, 10 of them with a patio or terrace. At a time when London had no minimum space standards, it was a pleasure to work to the standards of the VMSW (Flemish Company for Social Housing), giving us two-bed flats of 76m² total area, including 5m² of storage. The ground-floor flats are designed to lifetime-homes standards, so they have minimal circulation and a generous living–dining room at the heart, from which the main bedroom and the kitchen are entered.

We imagined the patios that perforate the building as outdoor rooms, extensions of the home. Housing design asks many things of the architect – logic, economy, ingenuity – but empathy is essential. When we draw a rectangle with lines coming outwards in perspective, we can't help but imagine that we're there, inhabiting this room that doesn't yet exist. By doing this, we try to take responsibility for what we make. So, our drawing of the roof terrace is an exploration of wanting your own space but liking contact with others; of looking down to the little communal garden and café terrace below; of feeling a kind of reflective distance from your life in the small town as you look over the pantiled roofs of the old rural inn to the medieval churchtower.

The first-floor terraces invite a kind of personal expression, as well as of course giving residents a generous balcony or an outdoor room to sit out in. The balance of privacy and openness seems to encourage people to occupy them in a relaxed way, to display a little bit of who they are.

We omitted the lift for cost reasons, so the first-floor apartments are for younger social tenants. The laminated timber beams of the low pitch roof are left exposed. Behind the steps, cranks and perforations, and the rooms of different minimum sizes, the beams and windows follow the same module of 550mm: they are like a background rhythm at the scale of the human body running throughout the scheme.

On the ground floor, the patios give good daylight and sunlight. The living–dining rooms are about 28m², with the kitchen beside the courtyard. While the living rooms have four doors in them, these are positioned in the corners to maximise the wallspace, and the large window to the patio has its cill at 600mm. These nuances ease furnishing in rooms that work quite hard.

Our priorities in spending the modest budget (about €1200/m²) were to stretch the building around the public space and to perforate the volume for daylight and external space for the apartments. As these

result in a lot of external envelope – the most expensive part of the building – the exterior is economical, bordering on austere: the cheapest brick, limewashed, stained wooden boarding, and purply-red clay pavers.

The flats connect to the courtyard through the recessed entrance porches on the ground floor and through the patios on the first floor – they are both deep thresholds. This depth comes from different things, it's not an end in itself, but seems fundamental to how people feel there. These thresholds between the home and the collective space, rather than acting as barriers or buffers, seem to work as invitations to sit out or to stand and talk. The courtyard also has its thresholds: a broad opening from the main street, and a narrow passage linking to the side street.

The new housing is fitted to the rustic scale of the old inn. But rather than copying its forms, we echoed the vernacular through the austere material palette. This sobriety underpins the generous scale and porous character of the apartments, and enabled the tailoring to the complex site. It's a modest but precise vision of the collective space of the small town – a shared outdoor room.

The process at Gistel took 12 years from our competition entry to practical completion. The inn and the square became separate projects by other architects; we had a subsidy refused because of the flat roofs; there were various delays for land purchase; and the site was suspended for two years, after the contractor for the square went bankrupt.

Thirteen units in 12 years is not a great build rate – but our client was stoical in the extreme. To paraphrase Pat Vansevenant's speech at the opening, 'If this took so long, it just shows we have to do many more of them'. In this perspective, where slow and small mistakes are preferable to fast and big ones, the issue is to multiply these small actions, not to scale or speed them up.

HOUSING IS FIRST OF ALL A WORK OF IMAGINING THE CITY

During the 12 years that we were building Gistel, we didn't stop trying to build housing in London – but we didn't make much headway. We drew up proposals for brownfield sites, for infill in housing estates, for estate renewal and large regeneration projects – for the public sector, the not-for-profit housing associations, the private-sector volume housebuilders. We have worked on proposals for hundreds of hectares, almost all of them sites in public ownership.

— In Stonebridge we won another Europan competition in 2005, and got planning consent for 122 apartments. This was part of the estate renewal of a high-rise 1970s estate. After the market crash, an approximation of our scheme by another architect is just completing 12 years later.

— At Ailsa Street in the Lea Valley, we prepared a masterplan in 2007 for compulsory purchase by the London Development Agency. The site is *still* vacant.

— In the wake of the financial crisis, the Olympic legacy shifted from high-density to low-rise and from fast payback to long returns. We prepared a strategy for public spaces and a masterplan for the strangely vertical crossroads at the centre of the site. The vision of slow stewardship seems to have been quietly dropped now that the market has heated up again.

— In Peckham, a scheme by another architect has just been awarded planning consent, 18 years on from our Europan design...

On these and other sites, we could have been cannier. But this strange inertia seems to affect many London projects, which are in a hurry one moment and on hold the next. You're under pressure to maximise the density because of the perceived land value, or the price that has been paid for it. So, you build over culverts and sewers and high-voltage cables – none of which speeds a project up – and haggle with neighbours over shifting boundaries and rights. You duck and dive through funding rounds and policy changes and electoral cycles. Is it that the sites aren't there to meet our housing needs? Or is it that the desire to take on complex sites isn't matched by the patience and experience at our disposal? Is it public land that is in short supply, or collective capacity?

Of course, the pressure of land value isn't confined to London, but can be felt across much of Europe, or at least in those parts that aren't shrinking. Cambridge has experienced quite intense economic growth, due to its knowledge-based industries. Private sector jobs have grown by 15 per cent over the past five years, while the population has increased by nearly 20 per cent in the last 20 years.

These trends have resulted in young and mobile post-graduate researchers finding themselves priced out of the housing market, threatening the University of Cambridge's ability to attract the best. In response, the university is developing a 3,000-home urban extension to the northwest of the city to deliver affordable housing for researchers and university employees – and it's on land previously in the Green Belt.

The university and local authority have agreed exceptionally high standards of sustainability for this extension of the city. These have been translated, most unusually for a city-edge development, into urban densities, with apartment buildings of four to five storeys in the central area. There is also sophisticated management of water and waste, measures to encourage cycling and reduce car dependency, and substantial collective services: a primary school, a community centre, a supermarket. It's a huge and complex undertaking for a university.

While large urban blocks of several hundred units make up most of the first phase of development, we have found ourselves designing a block of 27 apartments. This is a happy accident, the result of our collaboration with Maccreanor Lavington (MLA): we originally applied for a 300-unit plot, but succeeded in winning Lot 8 with 73 apartments, which we divided two-thirds to one-third. It's a tapering site about 80m long, narrowing from about 50m to 30m. What's interesting with this scale and division is that the project is small enough to be architecture, but large enough to also be a piece of urbanism.

The masterplan is based on streets and perimeter blocks, but the large plots tend to mean that building around the corner is an option rather than a necessity. This wasn't the case at the southern end of our site. Anyway, we wanted to support the character of this place as a city-in-the-making, and not a peripheral campus – and buildings on corners feel like a defining characteristic of cities. They're where you find pubs and, naturally, corner shops. So, we decided to reinforce this southwest facing corner by making the frontage continuous around the corner.

With Maccreanor Lavington, we pushed and pulled the volumes, simplifying them to form five-storey apartment blocks at either end, bookending a three-storey terrace. Since neither of us is afraid of repetition, the street front is calm and rhythmic. Their northern blocks are elegantly spartan, our southern block is more vertical, a little more staccato; the wall dissolves into windows with piers between.

At the front it's like a Parisian apartment block, with the windows of the main rooms repeating and wrapping round the corner. But at the back it's more like London housing, with an open stair and galleries. It's almost like it has been broken open, as if the harmonious front has been stripped away – like a doll's house or a ruin. This is a way of dealing with entering flats at different depths, with service riser doors, with the lift and stair that would otherwise just be lumps on the back. But it's also a reflection on the apartment building, on those cellular divisions that help us live together but apart.

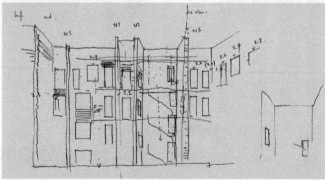

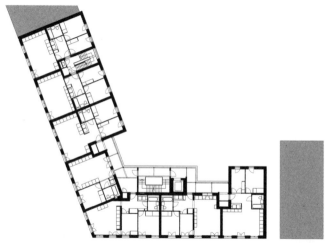

There are two main apartment types. The flats at the end of the gallery, and the walk-up flats in the terrace, are both 11m deep, with bedrooms at the back. The flats along the gallery are 7m deep; they distort and adapt around the corner. In the deeper flats the living–dining rooms have their long sides on the south and west faces. They are generously lit by French windows and get their breathing space from Juliet balconies. In the second bedrooms we have put double doors opening up to the hall or, at the front, a second door connecting to the living room. This is quite a common feature of apartment design in continental Europe (like the Brussels flats we got to know) – and it offers a nice flexibility of use. The second bedroom becomes part of the living area, as a study or a TV room, or belongs to the 'night' part of the house, as a place to sleep, according to the circumstances of the household.

We removed a passage planned at the side and widened the southern end of the block from 19m to 29m. The gardens and courts on the interior are more protected as a result. We displaced the passage to the ground-floor corner – cutting the pedestrian passage directly through the corner is a little act of transgression and a gesture in support of collective life. As the building sits just beyond the 'market square' and the shared services, we didn't have any public or commercial uses to fill the ground floor, and so concentrated what activity could be realistically anticipated and allowed for future possibilities. We widened the passage towards the corner, to form a covered room open on its sunny side, furnished with benches.

The idea is a bit like that long, low wall that forms such a magnificent bench on King's Parade, where you can sit and watch students and fellows parade or amble past. Or like one of those passages punched through a honey-coloured stone wall, linking one college court to the next. It's also a public interior, like a room whose fourth wall has been removed. We wanted to do it with a minimum of architecture, without columns or anything – so it's a big, strong horizontal cut, and a not insignificant cantilever.

We lined the outdoor room on the street corner in a deep red glazed brick, on both walls and soffit, giving it a strong sense of being an interior,

a contrast with the pale, warm brick on the exterior. The intensity of the red brick anticipates and links to the earthy brown brick of the stair and gallery. If you sit on the green oak bench, you look out as the street falls away to the west, along the swales and willows; or to the south where a small court opens up to the supermarket square. It's a nook with an outlook – intimate but open.

We always said that Gistel was a prototype, with test cases of all the difficult conditions in housing, or all those that required special treatment: the ground floor, the roof, outside corners, inside corners... Well, in Cambridge at least we got to repeat on first, second and third floors, with a lot of common conditions between flats. The fourth floor has a small variation, a set back at the east end, in anticipation of a four-storey neighbour to the east, while the ground floor has no apartments on the

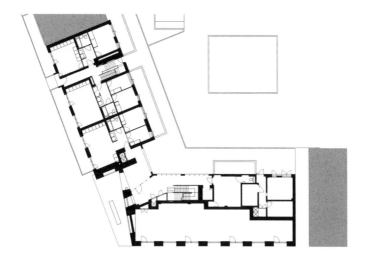

south side. We had a sub-station and bin stores to accommodate, and with the stair at the back, the ground floor on the main street felt too exposed to live in. So, we made a grand bike store – it was easier to build it into the fabric than as a stand-alone – which offers the possibility of future occupation. This place has moved from potato fields to streets in just a few years, and will need space for growth and change. Redundancy, or spare capacity, is what distinguishes the city from the campus, the housing estate or the business park. And that's what this ground floor offers: in time, it could become a bar, a shop or a shared room.

The stair and galleries are in filigree steel, and look out over the courtyard garden on the interior of the block, and the brick and concrete gallery of the north block by MLA. So the two 'bookends' not only shape the public spaces on their outer faces, their size and openness give a kind of immediacy to the long, narrow garden. Their scale holds its length in check, like a perspective correction. Because the galleries are generous enough to sit out on, they give a sense of the presence of other residents. Perhaps this slightly theatrical quality will help to shape the feeling that the garden is a common ground for the residents of these 73 flats – it will be interesting to see how the tenants respond.

In a way we have found ourselves responding to a greenfield in the same way we might have done with an existing site, which could be quite a wilful thing to do. But we'd see it more as a piece of opportunism, using the decisions that preceded us about plots and angles and drains to make something open and open-ended for our mobile young researchers and their families.

Back in London, in recent years the residential landscape and debate have shifted further still. High-rise has become more and more the default solution. We are presented almost daily with a vision of the city where everything is new and clean, where everyone is young and coupled. In this London of the near future, high-density building results in bustling public spaces, but the city seems to be a spectacle you look out on from behind a swathe of parkland or a moat of water – rather than something you are a part of. It's a revival – a distortion – of the modernist city, but without the progressive values.

One powerful white man's uninterrupted horizon of the city can be a more vulnerable person's permanent shade or blinding glare, or passage to the margins of the city. It is almost beyond satire...

We have witnessed the pressures on land values in local centres; one consequence has been the relocation of older people to the margins of London, out of sight, releasing central sites for higher-value investors. But this is an odd, desperate sort of city to be imagining and building. By 2035, the number of over-60s in London is expected to increase by nearly 50 per cent to almost two million, while the number of those aged over 80 will double – a 70 per cent increase on today's numbers.

It seems that now 80 per cent of us in Europe live in cities, we are starting to forget how to make them. Haven't we seen enough to question the emphasis on personal autonomy over mutual support; on the shiny new over the awkward old; on height at all costs over compact housing around believable collective spaces? Fortunately, that is what some determined organisations are committed to doing. And some of them find time and space for the kind of imagination that we try to bring to these things.

In Bermondsey, south London, we were presented with a new challenge: to imagine and design an 'almshouse for the twenty-first century'. In something like a virtuous triangle, the developer of a private residential tower in Bankside will fund affordable housing on a site owned by Southwark council. At Southwark's instigation, this will be built as 'extra care' housing for older people. It will be run in perpetuity by a local charity of 500 years' standing – USSC (United St Saviours). USSC run the Hopton Steet almshouse in Bankside, so they know the difference between an almshouse and an apartment building – and it is definitely an almshouse that they want.

The new almshouse will occupy the site of a vacated care home on Southwark Park Road, a meandering medieval lane that evolved into a Victorian high street with, among other things, a post office, shops, pubs, doctors' surgeries and the nearby 'Blue' marketplace. The area is an encounter of different models of London housing. The site is framed on three sides by a relatively intact Victorian neighbourhood, its northern edge is largely made up of post-war housing blocks.

One shocking irony of our high-rise, high-value, global city is that many more people are suffering desperately from loneliness and anxiety. It is understood to be a major killer of older people and those who feel isolated. Yet all of the models of older persons' housing we encountered – whether historical almshouses or new award-winning schemes – were in one way or another types of retreats. In each case, the shared room, chapel, hall or lounge tends to be set back from the street, often behind a fence and garden, and the residents have a concealed garden to sit in.

We spoke to one older man at an award-winning scheme in London. He was sitting in his wheelchair in the car park watching the busy street. Why was he not enjoying the carefully designed garden, we asked. The garden was very nice, he told us, but quite boring compared to all the interesting comings-and-goings on the street. So, the car park was a place to connect with the life of the city. In our proposals we responded to this insight and placed the shared room for residents right on the high street.

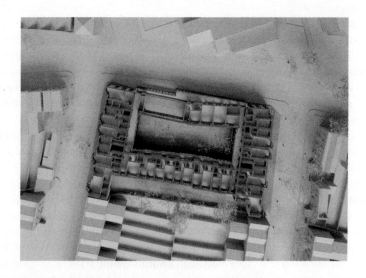

Apartments wrap around the other three edges of the site, defining a garden court and a small woodland garden behind.

The Board of USSC was quietly becoming frustrated that we did not show any drawings of what it all might look like, largely because we didn't know – we were struggling to find the essence of this more sociable and open almshouse. Then, during one of those conversations you have as you walk out of a meeting, the client mentioned that they funded many small organisations in Southwark. And this was the moment when confidence flowed into the project for us. Rather than seeing it solely as a place to live in with a warden and some healthcare provision, we could now imagine it also being a hosting place, supported and activated by local like-minded organisations as part of a broader social network.

The almshouse became porous to the high street, with a large cut illuminated by the garden court beyond. We enlarged the shared 'lounge' on the high street, making it double-height, bringing in more light and creating a stronger relationship between the street and garden court. We started to imagine that the lounge could also act as a modest café accessed by the public; it was suggested to us that it could be supported by a cookery school – staffed by residents and volunteers, replacing the traditional kitchen counter service. We thought this room could be used by local theatre groups and school groups to rehearse or perform; small music events could be accommodated and market days held to sell or exchange things. It became reasonable to believe that young and old could come together in a mutually beneficial way, sharing skills, thoughts, stories and support.

The garden court, around which the apartments are arranged, shares the dimensions and focus of the traditional coaching inn courts along the not-too-distant Borough High Street. The shared room opens onto the garden and allows visitors to sit and chat with each other and residents. The garden could be planted and maintained by the local gardening group.

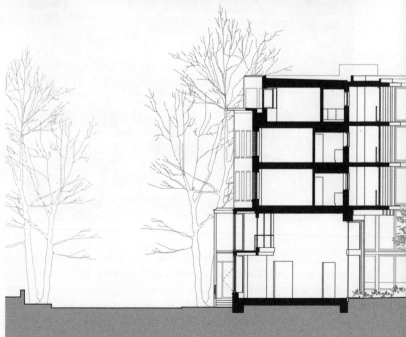

The south wing is two storeys high, ensuring reasonable sunlight into the garden court. Its roof is occupied by raised beds and a pergola for residents to grow vegetables and flowers. The north block is five storeys high, the top one set back. Each apartment opens onto the generous glazed gallery and overlooks the garden court. Residents can sit outside their kitchen with a friend or place a few potted plants to extend their homes into the shared deep balcony.

The materials proposed are robust but extend the textures, light and warmth of the garden deeper into the walkway. Large sliding glazed screens will naturally ventilate these shared spaces and let in the smells of the plants and the bird song. These are places that can open in the warm weather or act as winter gardens when it is cold, supporting sociability between residents as an alternative to the provision of small individual balconies.

Our re-interpretation of the traditional almshouse responds to the idea that older people live longer, are more active and have a lot to contribute to our urban centres. They do not all want to retire to some form of retreat away from the bustle of the city, but wish to remain as a vital source of continuity and commitment to the local places they have lived their lives in.

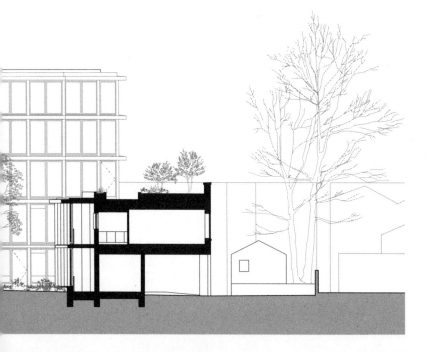

If we look at the places we've worked, or listen to the people who live in our apartments, or watch the character and tactics of the clients we've been lucky enough to work for, we start to understand a few things about the society and economy that we are a part of:
— we are living longer than preceding generations
— we live alone, or with one or two others
— we are mobile, and find work far from our families
— work is part of our identities, but it is uncertain and changeable
— we live densely packed in cities, depending on strangers, who depend on us
— these cities are old and tangled, an accumulation of expedient and contingent decisions

So, whether in an ancient Flemish town or in the fields outside of Cambridge, we have made a persistent effort to remember what is useful from previous iterations of our cities, freely reinvented within the forces of today's economy. In the porous volumes we have made, the unit loses its identity in a figurative composition. In our tortured plans, the logic of production is beaten and twisted, and the individual, the collective and the wider city are held in a dynamic balance. Embracing irregular sites, the binding figure is that of the collective space: multiple, active and fluid.

Our work in housing could be characterised as a kind of idealistic opportunism – an opportunism that needs those crunchy sites, and needs clients with deep reserves of patience, determination, empathy and a willingness to take risks, because that idea of mutuality means a lot to them.

When we design shared housing we don't know who will live there. In northwest Cambridge, *there* existed only as a ground and a few trees. These are huge gaps that as architects we fill as far as we can. Our imaginings prompt memories which spur new imaginings. If we adjust our focus, we find the point where architecture ends and life starts; where a corner is a place of crossed paths and slices of sunlight; a place to smoke, and a possibility for commerce; where light and calm and gardens are an invitation to pause, to drink amongst strangers, to learn from older generations; where a courtyard is a small theatre of collective life in which the roles of actors and spectators are blurred.

It's this inextricable relation of individual and collective, of the lived and the dreamed, of the assembled and the cultivated, that makes us ever more convinced that to design housing is first of all a work of imagining the city.

KATE MACINTOSH

Born in Rotherham in 1937, Kate Macintosh moved to Edinburgh from Cheshire at the age of 10 and studied at the city's College of Art. On graduation, she travelled and worked in Scandinavia before joining the office of Denys Lasdun in 1964 as a member of the design team of the National Theatre. The following year she joined the Architect's Department of the London Borough of Southwark, where she designed the Dawson Heights estate in Dulwich. In 1968 Macintosh moved to the London Borough of Lambeth, where she designed 269 Leigham Court Road, a sheltered housing development for the elderly. Her subsequent work in the public sector included sheltered housing, schools and buildings for the fire service commissioned by the counties of East Sussex and Hampshire. Later she joined her life-partner, George Finch, in private practice, winning a RIBA award, in 2005, for the design of an adventure playground in Weston, Southampton. 269 Leigham Court Road was awarded Grade II-listed status in 2015 and subsequently renamed Macintosh Court in honour of its architect.

Kate Macintosh's presentation is followed by a conversation with Rowan Moore, architecture critic for *The Observer* and author of *Slow Burn City* (2016) and *Why We Build* (2012). The talk took place at the office of Karakusevic Carson Architects on 22 June 2016.

I arrived at the Southwark Architect's Department in 1965, looking for some site experience after a year working with Denys Lasdun's office as the most junior member of the National Theatre team. And what I was presented with was this simply stupendous site off Overhill Road in Dulwich, one of a chain of hills that lie at a distance of about four miles south of the Thames – Tulse Hill, Streatham Hill, Gypsy Hill, Herne Hill. All have fabulous views. Here, looking north towards the city, you can see the docks, Primrose Hill and, on a clear day, Parliament Hill; to the south you have the North Downs and Crystal Palace.

The architectural influences are Park Hill, Sheffield by Jack Lynn and Ivor Smith, Lillington Gardens by Darbourne and Darke, Keeling House by Lasdun – all schemes that endeavour to express the individual dwelling within a unified totality. This was one of my ambitions. Wanting to exploit the views, I designed Dawson Heights as a pair of interlocking ziggurats, staggered to minimise the blocking of sun and view, and varying in height from twelve to three storeys. The tail of the two higher blocks flips around 90 degrees to enclose a central place on the scale of Bloomsbury Square.

Another driver towards a portion of high/medium-rise was the in-stability of the ground, slippery layers of London clay overlaid with spoil from the cutting for the nearby Crystal Palace railway. This made the foundations extremely costly – the structural advice was that even a single-storey structure would require piles to a depth of 30m. So economic logic dictated a restricted footprint. Of course, this unstable ground was the reason why the site was largely empty and available for construction.

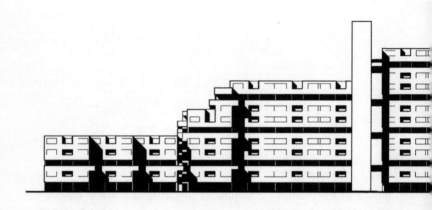

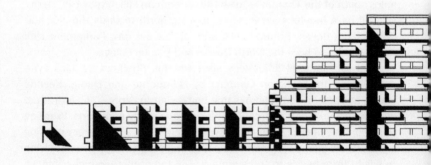

Dawson Heights, north and south elevations, 1966 © Kate Macintosh archive

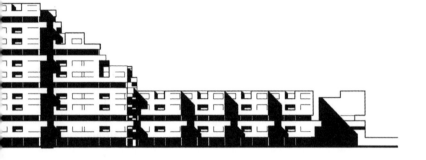

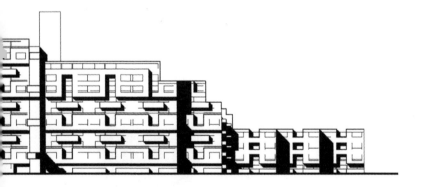

Dawson Heights was designed under the new standards for public housing set out in the Parker Morris Report, 'Homes for Today and Tomorrow', published in 1961 by Harold Macmillan's Conservative government. All the London boroughs voluntarily adopted these standards in 1964, when the main responsibility for housing was devolved from the LCC. Parker Morris didn't just establish minimum requirements for space (including storage space) in dwellings of various sizes, it freed up architects to plan housing in new ways. In the LCC, architects had been restricted to standard house-type plans. The dominant solution in most of its schemes was a mixed development putting smaller households in tower blocks and larger families in four- to five-storey walk-up blocks, with site layouts being somewhat arbitrary.

One of my criticisms of the LCC's standard mixed development scheme was that it created an artificial separation of people based on dwelling size. I wanted to encourage neighbourly relations by integrating families of different sizes and age groups, and so I devised this interlocking pattern whereby one-, two- and three-bedroom dwellings share access routes, the idea being that this is the sort of mix of people, with complementary strengths and needs, that you get in a community that has built up over many years. The four-bed units are entered from the lowest access deck.

An important influence on housing architecture at that time was the social study, *Family and Kinship in East London* (Michael Young and Peter Willmott, 1957), which looked at how the communities of the East End of London had remained cohesive, surviving even the horrendous experience of the Blitz, thanks to the strong social

● 4 bed units

● 3 bed units

● 2 bed units

● 1 bed units

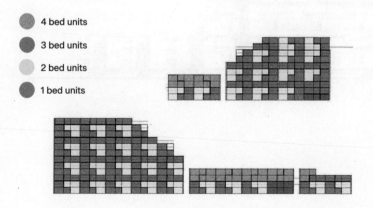

Dawson Heights, diagram of Blocks B1 and B2 showing the interlocking of dwellling types, as designed 1966 © Kate Macintosh archive

networks fostered by the two-up, two-down terraced housing. The thesis was that an awful lot of social capital had been lost in the process of erasing the street patterns and putting people into tower blocks – albeit in more spacious and hygienic flats. That was one of the reasons behind the development of streets in the sky and expressing the individual dwelling. I was trying to replicate the best characteristics of the terraced street.

The original design incorporated bridges that linked the two lowest parts of the complex to their sister block by continuing the lowest access deck between them, at a level one and a half storeys above ground. This not only allowed residents the maximum convenience of access to the nearest lift but also increased the sense of enclosure in the central space. To my mind the central conundrum in bulk housing is how to strike a balance between privacy and sociability. These kinds of quasi-public spaces, which the architect provides in an effort to encourage conviviality (it cannot be forced), are precisely the spaces that Thatcher's housing adviser, Alice Coleman, sought to eliminate in her drive to 'design out crime'. It was this strain of thought that led to the removal of the bridges after the scheme was sold to the Southern Housing Association, and to various other modifications that I regard as unfortunate – executed in an unsympathetic way.

One benefit of the change in ownership, however, was that the housing association designated the lower area of the slope (on which it's uneconomical to build) as a nature reserve open to the public. It's a big plus. Lots of people go there now, to watch birds and butterflies. It's also a favourite spot to view the fireworks on November 5th.

View of Dawson Heights from Dog Kennel Hill, *The Architects' Journal*, 25 April 1973
© Sam Lambert / About the Image

Dawson Heights, view from Overhill Road in 1973, soon after completion
© Robert Kirkman

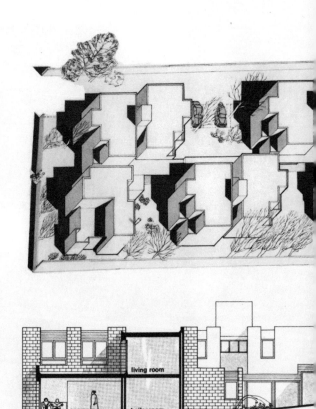

In 1969 I moved from Southwark to Lambeth, where I was given a much smaller scheme, for sheltered housing, that also served as a pilot project for metrication. Central government had issued an edict requiring all housing authorities to build a 'modular coordinated' scheme. Its stated aim was to improve the efficiency of house construction and encourage the standardisation of building materials, but it was also hoping, I think, to achieve those ends by other means after the demise of the big panel systems with the Ronan Point disaster. The stipulated module was 300mm by 300mm, which proved quite a challenge, given that the standard coordinating dimension for post-metric brick is 225mm. The only element that was suitable was dense masonry concrete block-work from Forticrete.

Sheltered housing, 269 Leigham Court Road, 1972, axonometric block plan and section east–west through common room and typical block © Kate Macintosh archive

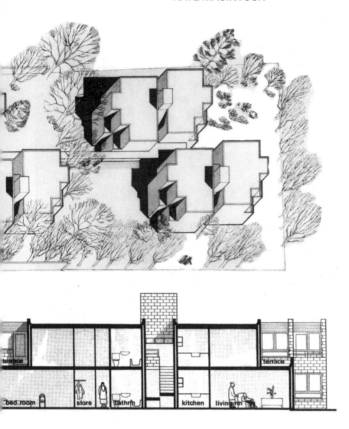

The site was a narrow suburban back lot that had once contained a substantial Edwardian house. Though it didn't offer much in the way of interesting activity, it did have the advantage of being a mature garden. A total of 44 flats are accommodated in five more or less identical cluster blocks plus two non-standard blocks. The brief called for one-person and two-person flats in the proportion of 3:1, which allowed me to produce setbacks at the first floor, giving all the flats at that level a south-facing roof terrace. The flats below all have semi-private outdoor space, formed by setbacks in the plan.

A typical cluster block comprises eight flats – four on each of the two floors. All the flats are oriented east or west; only the kitchens face north. The two remaining blocks, closest to the street, are arranged differently. One has a common room on the ground floor, and above it a large flat for a residential warden and family, where they can be aware of comings and goings but still retain privacy. The common room is oriented

Sheltered housing, 269 Leigham Court Road, 1972 © Kate Macintosh archive

towards the street, as is the shop in the other block (which I persuaded the housing manager to include for the convenience of residents and as a place of interchange with the local community). The location of these communal facilities near the entrance increases the opportunities for chance encounters between the residents. All these facilities are linked by a covered way, which I designed with an offset as it intersects with each of the cluster blocks, increasing in width at these points. I thought of the path as a stream of water, with little side eddies carving out spaces for people to linger and chat, or mill around, without obstructing the passage of others. I set out the buildings away from the existing trees, which were all retained.

Ted Hollamby was already a well-known figure in the profession when he became chief architect and planner for Lambeth in 1964. He had established a good reputation in the LCC for housing and schools, and had also been a member of the MARS (Modern Architectural Research) group – its influence could be seen in the way he set up the office, with its own R&D, landscape architecture and graphics sections. To ensure a high standard of structural design on this project he approached an associate from the MARS group, Ove Arup, and asked him to second a member of his staff, a structural engineer, to the Lambeth office.

This scheme, like many others developed during the Hollamby era, was threatened with demolition – the council wanted to dispose of the site to make way for a higher-density development. But to my enormous satisfaction a campaign of resistance to Lambeth's plans was launched by the residents, their friends and relatives, and the sheltered housing was Grade II-listed in 2015. This despite Lambeth having neglected it for 40 years.

Switching now to the work of George Finch, my late partner. George trained at the AA and after graduating in 1955 he went straight to work for the LCC Architect's Department, as many AA graduates did at that time. He was interviewed by the head of housing, Oliver Cox, who put him in a group still dominated by the old hands – mainly valuers and surveyors – in the hope that he would ginger them up. I certainly think he succeeded in making a difference. George's reputation today is largely defined by his tower blocks in North Lambeth, but he also designed the first two-storey family houses with gardens that came out of the LCC.

George moved to Lambeth in 1964, when Ted Hollamby recruited him along with Rosemary Stjernstedt. She was someone I looked up to, a pioneering architect who was also the first woman to be promoted to group leader in the LCC Architect's Department. At that time, the worst housing was in the north of the borough, where there was a shortage of land. So the idea was to surgically insert tower blocks into small sites to rehouse people from some of the worst slums, which could then be cleared to create larger sites. Another innovation was to set up an on-site production unit at Cotton Gardens to reduce delays in transportation from a remote factory and damage from the double-handling of panels. There are a total of eight of these heavily modelled big panel blocks in North Lambeth. Cotton Gardens has three: they were designed in collaboration with Ted Happold (who was then on the Ove Arup staff) and Neil Wates.

These are the only industrialised system buildings of which I am aware that achieved this measure of sculptural modelling and expression of the individual dwelling within the unified totality. All the blocks are identical above the ground floor, but the base of each contained a variety of different uses. Cotton Gardens had a play centre and a youth club. It also has a cluster of courtyard and two-storey dwellings, now under threat of demolition to allow for densification as part of the 'regeneration' of the estate. It is ironic to reflect that less than half a mile away as the crow flies, at Vauxhall, you have the 50-storey tower block designed by Broadway Malayan, two-thirds owned by non-doms, bought through secret off-shore companies. This accommodation stands almost empty most of the year, and that's regarded as ok, yet somehow it is seen as imperative to demolish this very popular housing that provides public open space not just for residents of the three tower blocks but for other local people.

Each of the point blocks at Cotton Gardens has 19 floors of housing, arranged as two-storey, two-bed maisonettes (eight every two floors), except at the top, where you have eight one-bed maisonettes with a double-height living space giving a definite termination to the block. This is one of George's themes. The maisonettes are single aspect and oriented east, west or south. The arrangement of the towers on the site is not orthogonal but twisted slightly to minimise overlooking and this gives a somewhat playful effect. They're 'dancing with each other', is how George described it.

George's next scheme – Lambeth Towers, opposite the Imperial War Museum – featured on the cover of the *RIBA Journal* in July 1965, which is when I first became aware of this talented architect. It is a complex design of 23 dual-aspect, two-bed maisonettes, in a cluster of four towers of varying heights, but rising to 11 storeys, with a one-bed flat at the top of each tower. The maisonettes have views onto the park and the museum to the north, and balconies on the south side. Ted Happold was the structural engineer and I think you can appreciate the degree of finesse that he brought to the scheme.

In George's sketch we can see once again a variety of different uses around the base. This drum with the split saucer roof was originally

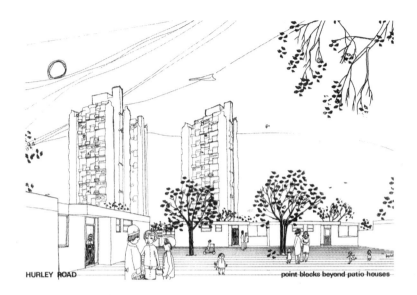

HURLEY ROAD   point blocks beyond patio houses

George Finch, perspectival view of Cotton Gardens with Knight's Walk in the foreground, from a report prepared for the London Borough of Lambeth, c 1966 © Kate Macintosh Archive

VIEW FROM THE PARK

George Finch, perspectival view of Lambeth Towers proposal, from a report prepared for the London Borough of Lambeth, 1967 © Kate Macintosh Archive

designed as an old folk's luncheon club and there are photos from the 1960s of people having a tea dance here. It is now a restaurant. There was also a registrar's office, as well as a doctors' group practice – there is still an administrative medical facility on the site.

The modifications made by leaseholders – past and present – show a lack of respect or appreciation for the quality of the buildings. For example, the elegant spiral of the fire-escape stair on the northern flank is now enclosed in an absolutely gross white plastic box. At ground level, King's Maths School has sploshed grey paint over the bush-hammered concrete and applied its coarse logo in mustard and black.

The name of the game in bulk housing is to concentrate use of the communal circulation, both so you can spend more money on the dwellings, but also to reduce the number of lift stops, making them more efficient. At Dawson Heights communal access is every third floor. Regardless of the dwelling size, all the living rooms face south (except for the flipped three- and four-storey tails of the tall blocks, which face east or west) and are half a level up or down from an access deck. And they all have a balcony.

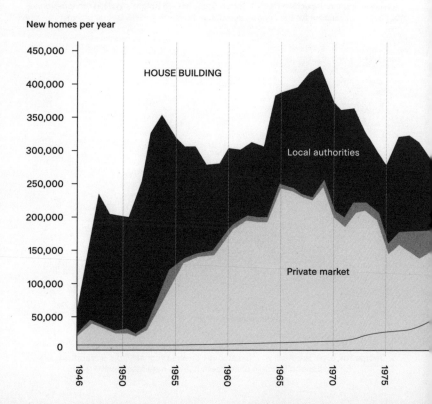

New homes per year

HOUSE BUILDING

Local authorities

Private market

In the Wates blocks, access is every second floor, with a narrower fire-escape corridor above that serves the front doors. Access is also every second floor at Lambeth Towers, where the cross-section is somewhat inspired by the scissor section of Le Corbusier's Unité d'habitation in Marseilles.

To finish I thought I'd show this graph adapted from James Meek's essay, 'Where Will We Live?', in the *London Review of Books*, which illustrates the steep decline in the production of local authority housing after Thatcher turned off the funding tap. She perhaps thought, naïvely, that the market would pick up the slack. But the market knows very well that with scarcity you get price inflation, which works in its interest. It is pertinent to reflect that in Scotland, where they have scrubbed right-to-buy and there has never been any stigma attached to renting, a survey found that the average disposable income is higher than across the rest of UK, for the simple reason that the cost of accommodation is lower.

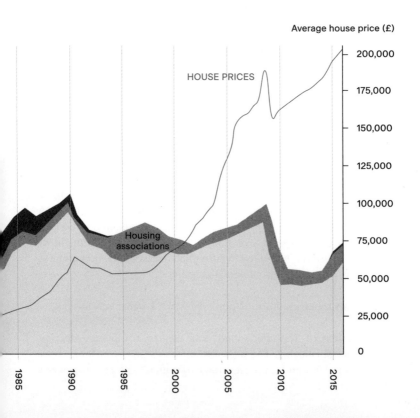

Rowan Moore: I would like to begin by asking about your background, Kate, and about how you came to be an architect and specifically an architect in public service, as I think this is a very important part of the story, before you reached the magic age of 27 and won Southwark's in-house competition for Dawson Heights.

Kate Macintosh: There's a bit of a Scottish theme here too. Both my parents were socialists. My father was a civil engineer and head of the direct labour organisation for Scottish Special Housing. This was a unique association set up after the First World War to deal with three problems – chronic unemployment, a shortage of skilled labour, and appalling housing conditions, particularly in Glasgow. My father had complete authority over who he hired and fired. He tendered competitively against outside contractors and won and finished jobs on time and within budget. He was an unusual man for his generation and an inspiration to me. It was he who suggested that architecture might fit the bill – I was always interested in something between the arts and the sciences that had some sort of social purpose.

RM Obviously those institutions don't exist in the same way today.

KM Oh no, one of Thatcher's first acts was to completely destroy Scottish Special Housing. The organisation was a one-stop shop. They purchased the land and employed their own architects and engineers.

They managed and maintained their own housing stock, with estates stretching from the Highlands and Islands down to the Borders. My father was always on the road.

RM Do you see that spirit of public social purpose around now?

KM It is much more alive in Scotland. Although they account for only 12 per cent of the UK population, they have built as much social housing in the last 10 years as the whole of the rest of the UK.

RM I didn't know that. Referring to the period you covered in your talk, the work you and George were doing was unusual, quite unlike the large, repetitive, industrialised estates being designed at the same time – Southwark's Aylesbury estate comes to mind. Did you find it difficult to convince others of what you were trying to do? Were there any internal tensions or arguments?

KM Right up until the collapse of Ronan Point in May 1968, central government was seeking to impose its preference for system-building, granting extra subsidies for using those methods. If you wanted to do something different, you had to make a good case. With Dawson Heights, we argued that industrialised building was inappropriate because the site conditions were so unique, both on account of the views and the unstable ground. Dawson was under construction when Ronan Point collapsed, but we didn't have to make any modifications – which was not the case with projects elsewhere.

RM After it was built did you get any favourable feedback about your design and how well the mixes of units worked?

KM I'm afraid I was rather preoccupied with other things afterwards. And there was a period when I was almost scared to acknowledge that I designed social housing, because immediately you got these scowls. So it was a huge relief to go back with Tom Cordell for the filming of 'Utopia London' (2008). Rather than being crucified, as I'd half-feared, I was lionised. People came up and threw their arms around me. Kids were jumping around, doing breakdancing. It was wonderful.

Tom Cordell actually interviewed Alice Coleman for the film. She lives not far from Dawson Heights and is still singing the same old tune – the one that goes 'the only form for decent housing is a detached or semidetached property with nice picket fences in the front and hedges to stop people peering in through the net curtains'.

RM Is there anything you'd do differently now? Any change you'd make, with the benefit of hindsight?

KM One thing is security at the points of entry. We were unrealistically optimistic in those days, thinking we were heading for a classless society. It was a different world before the drug culture came in. I understand Dawson Heights went through a bad patch when these things were an issue, but I don't agree with the Alice Coleman doctrine that says architecture produces crime. What produces crime is inequality and exclusion from opportunity. Of course under Thatcher local authorities were deliberately starved of funds – central government took an 80 per cent cut of the rents – so they were unable to carry out the most basic maintenance, and tenants increasingly opted to transfer ownership to the housing associations. In my view housing associations should have resisted right-to-buy. They were set up specifically to provide housing for the needy and now they are in breach of their founding fathers' ethos. And as their portfolios shrink, so does their ability to raise money to continue their operation. They have effectively bowed to legalised larceny by the government.

RM Which brings us to the present. Do you have any views about how best to tackle the current housing crisis?

KM I actually have rather a long list. A good starting point would be to equalise VAT between renovation and new build: new build is currently VAT exempt, so it's cheaper to knock down and start again. Then I would introduce land value taxation to stop land banking. Volume house builders have planning consent on a vast amount of land, which they're not developing – they don't need to, its value goes up without them doing a single thing. The same goes for the supermarkets. They could be forced to build or sell up. The whole question of housing comes down to land and ownership (Karl Marx said, failing all else, if revolution didn't occur spontaneously, land value taxation would be capitalism's last chance to redeem itself). I would also pass the kind of legislation they have in Norway and Australia to prevent non-doms from purchasing a single acre of UK land. When public land does come up for sale it should first be offered locally, as is the case in Germany.

Q1 The idea of participation has changed hugely since the 1970s. When you were designing projects, did you have any contact with the future residents? And if so, how did that relationship go?

KM I may sound like I'm eulogising about that time, but actually there were defects. In many local authorities chief officers would jealously guard their silos of power. The housing manager at Southwark was a case in point. Together with some colleagues I carried out research into life in a slab block of flats in Camberwell. We knocked on doors and talked to people about how they liked living there. They told us they felt very restricted: they weren't allowed any pets, or anything on their escape balconies – any expression of individuality at all. It was utterly institutional. Lambeth was much better. Ralph Erskine and his team at the Byker estate showed how to carry out genuine consultation – unlike most local authorities today, which go through a formulaic pretence.

Q2 We're working with the London Borough of Camden. What do you think the role of the local authority should be in social housing provision, moving forward?

KM I lament greatly the loss of a large body of expertise, represented not just by in-house architects but also by client bodies in education, social services and so on. Now, when the commissioning of buildings is such a fragmented business, they apparently feel they have to reinvent the wheel – the corporate store of experience and wisdom has been dissipated. I hope it can be retrieved. I feel it could be, given the political will, and the ingenuity of the profession. And I know that Camden, Islington and Croydon are beginning to do this.

Q3 Lots of your examples are amazing buildings in sensitive environments. What was the process of getting them through planning? Even if it was internal, who were you answering to? And what do we do today, about all the obstacles put in the way of work that is aesthetically ambitious?

KM I must admit I never had any problems with planners, other than with a small private job. When I was operating in London a very high proportion of planners were also capable architects, whereas the next generation of planners had a first qualification as geographers or surveyors and they didn't seem to get much architectural training. My impression is that the dumbing down is not the fault of planners but has a lot to do with design-and-build, PFI and PPP. Once planning is granted, the architect hands over to the developer – your power is truncated. Gone are the days when an architect could go onto site and say 'That's not up to standard, take it down.' It would drive me crazy.

Q4 I am in temporary accommodation in Elephant and Castle, which is being redeveloped by Lendlease in partnership with Southwark council. I was in the Heygate estate, which was demolished though there was nothing wrong with it. I have been to meetings and no one took any notice of us. To me, the whole thing is a scam and I wonder what you think about it?

KM The housing manager at Southwark was heard to say that he wasn't interested in any site that couldn't support at least 2,000 dwellings. So he was into economies of scale. Putting aside the architecture, which was not all that bad, I think this explains what went wrong at Heygate and Aylesbury Road in the 1970s. When you clear such a large area it causes huge social destruction. You can promise people they will be rehoused in the same area, but those with skills will go where there are opportunities, as they did to Milton Keynes and so on. The people left to be rehoused are the vulnerable and the needy. It's like in a forest – clear too large an area it cannot reseed itself. It's a tragedy that 40 years on, just as the community has got itself together, we are going through it all again, because of pressure coming from central government and councils being strapped for cash. The same thing is happening in Lambeth. They want to pull down Central Hill, an absolutely brilliant scheme designed by Rosemary Stjernstedt, under Ted Hollamby. Though I sympathise with their predicament, it is a great irony that many of these boroughs are Labour-controlled and they're conducting a sort of patricide, devouring the product of their own best tradition.

Q5 I wonder if you could say something about your own training as an architect. To have designed your schemes when you were so young would have required not only a lot of skill and confidence but also an assurance that you would be given the means to realise your ideas – whereas now I feel there is little trust in architects to see their work through. As you said, it is left to contractors and accountants to realise the end product.

KM I trained in architecture at Edinburgh College of Art and did my year out with Robert Matthew's Edinburgh office, which was a great environment. I did some holiday work with the LCC, where there was a relatively a high number of women architects, then after graduating I won a British Council scholarship to Poland – which was quite interesting though I can't say I did much architecture. I worked for two years in Scandinavia, in part because I knew that women architects were not regarded as oddities there, so I came back bursting with self-confidence, but very little site experience. I suppose the Edinburgh school was quite hands-on, though. I was careful to really look into constructional details and draw them meticulously. I'd done this ever since a tutor had told me after a crit: 'Miss Macintosh, we find that women tend to be good at colour and things like that but they are not terribly practical, how about thinking about something like interior design?' Luckily for me I was (and am) a stubborn individual and I thought, 'Right, I'll bloody well show them!'

In my presentation in June 2016 I talked about the threat to demolish Knight's Walk, the low-rise complex set in George Finch's Cotton Gardens estate. Since then, despite a vigorous campaign led mainly by the leaseholders, planning permission has been granted for the demolition of eight of the patio houses – about a 40 per cent attrition rate. Work is due to begin on site in January 2019: readers are encouraged to visit the scheme before its mutilation. As of January 2018 campaigns continue, against the odds, to resist the destruction of two other fine schemes from the Hollamby years: Cressingham Gardens and Central Hill. Both have had listing applications rejected.

However the great game-changing event, in June 2017, was the Grenfell Tower disaster, which threw into stark relief the dysfunctionality of all levels of government and their abrogation of responsibility for basic obligations of care. To take just one aspect of this disaster, the London Fire Brigades Union stated that their rescue efforts were hampered by delays in sending relief crews. Ten fire stations in the capital had closed in January 2014, with the loss of 552 fire-fighters and 14 fire engines. The fire service had warned at the time that this cost-cutting would put lives at risk. Grenfell Tower burned 350 years after the London Rebuilding Act of 1667, which attempted to eradicate the risks that had led to the Great Fire of London. This legislation was scrapped in 2012 by the coalition government.

Another aspect, illustrating the long-term erosion of any respect for professionalism and for architects in particular, was the peripheral position of the consultant architect, at the upper end of a minor tributary into the byzantine delta of confused responsibilities that passed for the management structure of this ill-fated, over-clad contract. The disregard of their advice to use a non-flammable panel, at slightly higher cost, vividly illustrates the consequences of making profit the overriding objective.

Then there was the outsourcing of the estate's management to the so-called 'Tenant Management Organisation', which turned a deaf ear to all the tenants' warnings of an impending major disaster, as they observed at first-hand the corner-cutting and the failures of maintenance.

In July 2017 I was called by ASH (Architects for Social Housing) to a tenants' meeting at Cotton Gardens, in a bid to reassure residents that the blocks were safely designed. The tenants had not received even the most rudimentary advice on the need to ensure that door-closers were functioning and that there were no obstructions on the dedicated escape routes accessed from their bedroom floors. Another casualty of the government's drive to commodify everything is the termination of free advice on fire-prevention from the fire brigade.

This sense of there being no reliable support structure – every man and woman for themselves – is precisely what the neo-liberal agenda wishes to encourage, so severing the bonds of mutual regard that bind society into a cohesive whole. If they succeed in this, they can let rip, with nothing to get in their way as they go on clearing social housing and handing over acres of public land to Lendlease and all the other hungry developers now circling the fold like wolves.

London, 13 January 2018

ACKNOWLEGEMENTS

This book, and the lectures on which it is based, would not have been possible without the generous support of a number of people and institutions: Jane Alison and Catherine Ince at the Barbican; Mike Althorpe at Karakusevic Carson Architects; Funto Thompson at Peter Barber Architects; the photographer Morley von Sternberg; Diego Leal at the Royal Geographical Society; Sarah Handelman at the AA; Eleanor Howard, Matthew Bovingdon-Downe, Rhea Martin and their brilliant team of Architecture Foundation volunteers. We would particularly like to thank Paul Karakusevic and Rowan Moore for chairing the Neave Brown and Kate Macintosh talks and Pamela Johnston and Rosa Nussbaum for their tireless and inspired work on the book's editing and design.

Project Interrupted represents The Architecture Foundation's first experiment in self-publishing. The production costs have been funded by over 1,000 companies and individuals who pre-ordered the publication in response to a month-long crowdfunding campaign. We are enormously grateful to everyone who supported the book in this way and particularly to those who backed it at the Friend, Sponsor and Patron levels. We are now keen to test the wider application of this economic model and welcome proposals for other architecture books that we can help bring to publication.

The Architecture Foundation receives no public subsidy and is reliant to a great extent on the financial backing of the many supporters whose names are listed at architecturefoundation.org.uk

COLOPHON

Publisher
The Architecture Foundation
Royal College of Art
Kensington Gore
London SW7 2EU
T +44 (0)20 7186 0279
architecturefoundation.org.uk

The Architecture Foundation
Ellis Woodman, Director
Phineas Harper, Deputy Director
Matea Vlaskalic, Office Manager

Editor
Pamela Johnston

Graphic Design
Rosa Nussbaum

Printing
Graphius

Type
Beausite, Fatype

Contents © 2018 The Architecture Foundation
and the Authors

ISBN 978-1-9996462-0-2

The Architectural Foundation
is a Registered Charity No 1006361
and a Company limited by guarantee
Registered in England No 02661352
Registered office as above